FAST & SIMPLE
gluten-free

FAST & SIMPLE
gluten-free

30 MINUTES OR LESS TO FRESH AND CLASSIC FAVORITES

✻ Gretchen F. Brown, R.D. ✻

FAIR WINDS
PRESS
BEVERLY, MASSACHUSETTS

© 2012 Fair Winds Press
Text © 2012 Gretchen Brown

First published in the USA in 2012 by
Fair Winds Press, a member of
Quayside Publishing Group
100 Cummings Center
Suite 406-L
Beverly, MA 01915-6101
www.fairwindspress.com

16 15 14   4 5

ISBN: 978-1-59233-524-4

Digital edition published in 2012
eISBN-13: 978-1-61058-631-3

Library of Congress Cataloging-in-Publication Data available

Book and cover design by Rita Sowins / Sowins Design

Photography by Gretchen Brown

Printed and bound in China

The information in this book is for educational purposes only. It is not intended to replace the advice of a physician or medical practitioner. Please see your health care provider before beginning any new health program.

For my momma, who taught
me to love, laugh, and eat.

Contents

Introduction

For as long as I can remember, I have loved to be in the kitchen. It is a place of nourishment for our bodies, souls, and minds. The food we serve from our kitchens turns strangers into friends; evokes memories of people, places, and experiences; brings joy and light to our senses; and nourishes and energizes us throughout our lives.

My love affair with food started in my mother's kitchen, extended through college in Food Science kitchens as a dietetics student, landed me in a test kitchen for a major magazine and cookbook publishing house, and then allowed me to turn my home kitchen into my "office" as a freelance recipe developer, food stylist, and food photographer.

You can imagine my shock and disappointment to learn after countless years of constant stomach pains, fatigue, and other health problems that the problem was coming from my own kitchen—specifically, the gluten in my food. The registered dietitian in me recognized the symptoms, but the food lover in me was in mourning. Suddenly my kitchen was a foreign, scary place to be. I mentally ripped all the baking chapters out of my many cookbooks and struggled to accept that all pizzas, baked goods, and sandwich breads I could safely consume for the rest of my life would come from frozen, overpriced packages.

But wait . . . I loved my kitchen. My will and my taste buds weren't going to settle. Even though we are accustomed to using gluten-filled wheat flour—we've been cooking and baking that way for thousands of years—that certainly doesn't mean it is the only option. It is just a matter of changing our way of thinking. And it is so much easier to think clearly and embrace changes when you physically feel so much better.

Without gluten, not only did I not feel sick every single day, but I was also becoming a pioneer in a new chapter of the book on food. Suddenly it was not about what I was not allowed to eat, but about what I could eat and how to prepare the dishes I knew and loved in a brand new way. I was creating recipes just as comforting, mouthwatering, and soul-feeding as always, only now prepared with a few different ingredients on the list.

This is precisely why I have written this book. Food is one of the biggest parts of our lives—it is a big part of our every day. And as gluten-free eaters, we need to know we can still hold on to what we crave and love from our kitchens. We, too, deserve to have foods that make us sing, foods that still instantly bring back those old memories, and foods that awaken and delight our senses. None of the beauty and wonder of food needs to be whitewashed over because gluten has been removed from it.

Bon appétit!

CHAPTER 1

Gluten-Free Basics

BEFORE WE DELVE INTO THE RECIPES, LET'S FIRST TALK ABOUT THIS LITTLE DEVIL, GLUTEN.

Gluten is a protein found in some grains, including wheat, rye, and barley. This would include traditional breads, pastas, baked goods, and some other unsuspecting foods, like soy sauce, salad dressings, beers, and licorice candies, for example. For some people, this little protein is powerful enough to cause a whole spectrum of symptoms and problems, ranging from migraines and skin rashes to severe gastrointestinal illness. The diagnoses related to gluten can come in a few forms, which I will outline briefly here.

Celiac disease (CD) is a lifelong autoimmune disease; therefore, it is more commonly seen in people who have or have had family members with other autoimmune diseases, such as type 1 diabetes, rheumatoid arthritis, or thyroid disease. When someone with celiac disease ingests gluten, it creates a toxic physical reaction, causing the body to attack its normal tissues, damaging the villi of the small intestine and preventing the absorption of nutrients. A strict gluten-free diet is required to allow the body to heal and prevent further damage and disease. As many as 3 million Americans have CD, which is estimated at 1 in 133 people; possibly even 1 in 100. Because of the broad spectrum of approximately 250 symptoms, a tremendous number of people go undiagnosed, even as long as eleven years from the first onset of symptoms.

Non-celiac gluten sensitivity (NCGS) is a bit different. Unlike celiac disease, there is no damage done to the intestine when gluten is ingested, therefore causing no nutritional deficiency. On the other hand, gluten ingestion does cause similar gastrointestinal pains and discomfort and can affect other parts of the body as well. It is estimated that 15 percent of Americans suffer from NCGS. Like celiac disease, a strict gluten-free diet is mandatory to remain healthy.

There are other groups of people who also must adhere to a strict gluten-free diet as well, including those who have an allergic histamine response to gluten that may cause rashes, swelling, hives, and even anaphylactic shock and those with gluten-related diseases and disorders, such as Meniere's disease, Raynaud's disease, autism, and a host of others conditions.

➡ HOW TO EAT

Now, let's talk about what *cannot* be eaten. The following list outlines the major gluten culprits (note that this list is not all-inclusive; many products may contain gluten without you realizing, so always read ingredient labels carefully!):

• Wheat	• Bulgur	• Farina	• Seitan
• Wheat bran	• Barley	• Faro	• Semolina
• Wheat germ	• Barley malt	• Graham	• Spelt
• Wheat oil	• Couscous	• Kamut	• Triticale
• Cream of wheat	• Durum	• Matzo	
• Cracked wheat	• Einkorn	• Rye	

It is also extremely important to avoid bulk bins of foods, toasters, pans, and kitchen equipment shared with products that contain gluten, as well as naturally gluten-free foods that may have been processed in a factory that also processes foods with gluten. All of these open up opportunities for cross-contamination, which is an enormous concern for most people avoiding gluten. Most important, always check labels so you can be confident that what you are eating is indeed gluten-free. Always.

It's truly more fun to talk about what you *can* eat when you begin eating gluten-free. Upon discovering gluten-free doughnuts, cupcakes, and brownies, however, it can be hard to remember it isn't necessary to eat them just because you can. The dietitian in me must remind you that occasional sweet treats and carbohydrate-filled snacks are just fine, but eating an entire bag of gluten-free cookies isn't any better for your waistline, your blood sugar, or your general health than if they were made with wheat. Trust me, my sweet tooth is rather insatiable, and I've most certainly included plenty of mouthwatering, heavenly dessert recipes in this book. But it's still important to remember to include lots of protein, vegetables, fruits, and gluten-free whole grains and flours in your daily meals.

➡ FLOUR, FLOUR, EVERYWHERE

We gluten-free folks have a tremendous number of exciting gluten-free flours at our fingertips. These flours impart flavors and textures that many people would never consider because they're so accustomed to using all-purpose wheat flour, so consider it an opportunity!

Gluten-free flours are divided into two categories: grains and starches. Because wheat flour naturally contains both, it is important to mix gluten-free grain flours and gluten-free starches when baking.

Here are a few of my favorite grain flours and starches. This list in no way covers all of the exciting gluten-free options available, but it is merely a compilation of the ones I find myself using the most.

<<< Grain Flours >>>

BROWN RICE FLOUR: Because this flour is milled from whole-grain brown rice, it is much higher in protein, fiber, and nutrients than its white rice counterpart. It is rather dense and heavy, but it mixes really well with other flours. It is available in a range of textures, from superfine to coarse. I use superfine flour to avoid any grittiness the coarser grinds can create in baked goods.

SORGHUM FLOUR: Sorghum flour is also milled from the whole grain, providing good fiber and protein. It's a heavy flour, but its flavor and color are relatively neutral, so it works really well in gluten-free baking.

BUCKWHEAT FLOUR: Despite its name, buckwheat contains no wheat. However, its dark color, heavy texture, and higher protein and fiber amounts resemble whole-wheat flour. It has a strong, hearty flavor that blends well with other milder flours.

COCONUT FLOUR: Coconut flour is a delightful addition to a gluten-free pantry. It is high in protein and fiber, low in carbohydrates, and imparts a mild, sweet, coconutty richness and texture. It likes to absorb liquid more than other flours, however, and therefore doesn't substitute into flour blends as well.

NUT FLOURS: These flours are made from grinding raw nuts to a fine powder. Most commonly seen is almond flour, but others include hazelnut, chestnut, macadamia, and pistachio flours. These flours are very high in protein and healthy fats and provide a distinctive nutty flavor.

BEAN FLOURS: Bean flours are another high-protein and high-fiber option. Most beans flours are milled from chickpeas and/or fava beans. These flours have a very noticeable earthy, beany flavor that some people find unpleasant. They work best when mixed with other flours in a blend.

TEFF FLOUR: Teff is an ancient Ethiopian grain that is high in fiber and iron. Nutritionally, it's even considered a complete protein. The whole, tiny grain is ground to make teff flour, which blends beautifully into baked goods and imparts a slightly sweet, slightly nutty flavor.

CORN FLOUR: Corn flour is finely ground dried corn, very different from cornmeal (which is a much coarser grind) and cornstarch (see page 14). Corn flour is a whole-grain, heavy flour that works particularly well with savory dishes.

OAT FLOUR: Oat flour is made from finely grinding whole oats. It adds a fantastic texture and valuable structure to baked goods. Always confirm that oats and oat flours are certified gluten-free. Oats are frequently processed in facilities that also process wheat, so chances of cross-contamination are very high. There are, however, several companies that are certified gluten-free.

SWEET RICE FLOUR: This flour is also called glutinous rice flour, though it contains no gluten. "Glutinous" actually refers to its sticky, starchy properties, making sweet rice flour one of the starchiest of the grains. (Since it's more starchy than it is grainy, I count it as a starch when I use it in a blend.) It is milled from short-grain white rice, and the high starch content provides a fantastic chewiness to baked goods.

<<< Starches >>>

ARROWROOT: Arrowroot is a fine, white powder extracted from arrowroot tubers that is similar to cornstarch in flavor, appearance, and function. It is a good thickener for sauces, and it also makes a nice crisp crumb when used in baking.

CORNSTARCH: One of the more popular starches, cornstarch has found its way into most of our pantries already. In addition to being a great thickening agent, this fine, white powder is so light in texture that it adds delicateness to baked goods.

POTATO STARCH: Potato starch is a white powder that is made from the starch of dehydrated potatoes. This starch also works very well in baked goods, adding softness to gluten-free products. It is very different from potato flour, which is made from the whole potato and imparts more of a "potato" flavor.

TAPIOCA STARCH/FLOUR: Tapioca starch (also called "tapioca flour") is derived from the roots of the cassava plant. It is a fantastic thickener and produces a clear gel. When used in gluten-free baking, it imparts a desirable chewy texture and added structure.

>>> Making a Blend >>>

Unlike all-purpose wheat flour, which naturally contains both grain and starch, gluten-free "all-purpose" flour requires a mix of flours to achieve this same result. My version is a mix of 50 percent grain and 50 percent starch. I find this ratio works best for "all purposes" and is a constant in my kitchen. This is also the flour I use most commonly in recipes I post on Kumquat, my gluten-free food blog (www.kumquatblog.com).

Depending upon what you wish your final product to look and taste like, the flours are mostly interchangeable within their category (grain or starch). For example, you can substitute teff flour for sorghum flour or cornstarch for arrowroot. For a more "whole grain" flavor and texture, the percentages can be increased in favor of the grains; just be sure to include at least 20 percent starches.

✴ QUICK TIP: REMEMBER THE MAGIC NUMBER ✴

If you have a kitchen scale and are interested in adapting recipes outside of this book that aren't gluten-free, it's helpful to keep in mind that one cup of wheat flour weighs approximately 140 grams. So when you substitute in your gluten-free flour, be sure to keep the cup-for-cup gram weight is the same.

Kumquat's Gluten-Free All-Purpose Flour Blend

YIELD: ABOUT 8 CUPS (1 KG)

2⅓ cups (about 300 grams) superfine brown rice flour
2 cups (about 200 grams) sorghum flour
1 cup (about 150 grams) sweet rice flour
1 cup (about 150 grams) potato starch
1 cup (about 100 grams) arrowroot starch
¾ cup (about 100 grams) cornstarch

Place all the ingredients in a large bowl or storage container. Stir or whisk well to combine.

Store in the refrigerator. Excess, unblended flours may be stored in your freezer for their longest shelf life and to keep the oils in the flours from becoming rancid.

>>> A Word on Binding Agents <<<

The last important thing to consider when baking gluten-free is a binding agent. Gluten is a structural protein. The reason you knead bread dough and don't manhandle a piecrust when using wheat flour is because of gluten. Whether you want more gluten to support the rise of a yeast bread or less gluten to result in a tender, flaky crust, you can still manipulate the structure of the baked good because it contains gluten. Remove the gluten from that baked good and you are left needing to add something to give it the desired structure.

Xanthan gums and guar gums are very frequently added to gluten-free baked products for this purpose. They act as a binding agent, adding structure in the place of gluten. More and more people are realizing, however, that these gums can cause gastrointestinal upset. After years of tummy pains, the last thing I want is more tummy pains. Therefore, I do not use gums in my baking, and you will find no gums required in the recipes in this book.

As an alternative, ground golden flaxseeds make a fantastic binder (and they also work as an egg substitute). When combined with warm water, they form a viscous, gluey mixture that adds structure to gluten-free baked goods. They are also a great source of omega-3 fatty acids and fiber. While I do not add them to my all-purpose flour blend—not all baked goods need the structural assistance—I do use them for cakes, breads, scones, biscuits, and other baked goods that need to hold their shape.

>>> Scale Success >>>

Lastly, I must share a secret with you that has entirely changed baking in my kitchen. It's a kitchen scale. I strongly encourage you to invest in and use the weight measurement of flours in this book before opting for the cup measures. Weighing flours is mandatory for success when baking gluten-free. I can't stress that enough. A cup of each different flour will result in a completely different weight on the scale; one cup of sweet rice flour will weigh much less than a cup of coconut flour, for example. So while flours are interchangeable in a blend or a recipe, if you do substitute, stick to the scale weights, which I've provided on all recipes, and not necessarily the cup measures. If you must use cup measures, stir the flour, spoon it into cups, and level it off with a knife or spatula.

➡ FAST & SIMPLE FOR YOU

These days, we all have so many tasks to tend to, children to drive here and there and jobs that consume much of the day. But at the end of that day, we still deserve good food. The recipes in this book will take you only 30 minutes from the time the ingredients hit your counter to when they grace the dinner table. The last chapter of the book is the only exception to this rule, as it includes some delightful gluten-free baking recipes that are fast and simple, but will require additional "hands-off" time for baking in the oven. In my opinion, no gluten-free cookbook would be complete without recipes for cakes, muffins, cookies, and brownies; therefore, I couldn't leave them out of this one! Trust me: Even if you have to wait a little longer than 30 minutes, I'm certain you'll agree they're worth it!

To enjoy the quickest, most successful experience with these recipes, I encourage you to practice *mise en place*, the French term for "everything in place." This refers to organizing all ingredients and equipment needed before beginning to cook, and it's a great concept to practice at any time, but definitely when attempting to prepare meals quickly.

I want these recipes to fill you with courage in your gluten-free kitchen and confidence that gluten-free cooking really can be fast, easy, and delicious. May they make your hearts happy, your bodies healthy, and your tummies full!

CHAPTER **2**

Breakfasts to Jumpstart the Day

BREAKFAST IS THE BEST. Not only does it involve coffee, which is always a hit for me, but the smells of bacon, cheesy eggs, pancakes, and warm cereals are sure to lure me from my warm bed. For those people who cannot eat gluten, however, breakfast can seem like a bit of a disappointment at first, as many of those delicious foods we loved to eat in the mornings were full of gluten. But all breakfast disappointments end here! Pancakes, crêpes, griddle cakes, granolas, and much more can be back on your gluten-free plate in minutes. And your taste buds won't feel like they're missing a thing!

Eggs en Cocotte

Also called "shirred eggs," baked eggs are a lovely, easy, and delicious way to enjoy your morning protein. This one adds vitamin-packed Swiss chard, earthy mushrooms, and nutty Parmesan cheese to create a fantastic savory combination.

½ cup (80 g) chopped onion
1 clove garlic, minced
1 tablespoon (14 g) butter
1 cup (70 g) sliced mushrooms
1 cup (67 g) chopped Swiss chard
1 tablespoon (2.4 g) fresh chopped
   thyme
¼ teaspoon salt, divided
¼ teaspoon black pepper, divided
4 tablespoons (20 g) grated Parmesan
   cheese, divided
4 large eggs
4 teaspoons (20 ml) heavy cream,
   divided

Preheat oven to 350°F (180°C, or gas mark 4).

Cook the onion and garlic in butter in a large skillet over medium-high heat for 3 minutes. Add the mushrooms and Swiss chard and cook for 3 minutes. Stir in the thyme, ⅛ teaspoon salt, and ⅛ teaspoon pepper.

Place 4 (5-ounce, or 150 ml) ramekins on a baking sheet. Divide the mushroom mixture evenly among the ramekins. Sprinkle 1 tablespoon (5 g) grated Parmesan into each ramekin. Crack one egg into each ramekin. Pour 1 teaspoon (5 ml) heavy cream on the top of each egg; sprinkle evenly with remaining salt and pepper.

Bake for 5 minutes. Turn broiler on high, move the baking sheet to a rack 6 inches (15 cm) from heat, and broil for 3 minutes or until the whites of the eggs are just set. (Yolks should be runny. If this is not to your liking, continue to cook to desired degree of doneness.)

Boursin Omelet with Tomatoes & Spinach

YIELD: 2 SERVINGS

Wow, wow, oh, wow. This omelet is good. A friend of mine said it best: "Swiss and Boursin should get married and have a baby." If they did, their perfect love child would taste something like this omelet. It's a fresh, decadent, easy way to start your day, or end it!

5 large eggs

2 tablespoons (30 ml) milk or milk alternative

¼ teaspoon salt

⅛ teaspoon black pepper

2 teaspoons canola oil, divided

2.6 ounces (75 g) garlic and herbs spreadable cheese (such as Boursin), divided

½ cup (15 g) fresh spinach leaves, divided

½ cup (90 g) chopped tomatoes, divided

1 cup (110 g) shredded Swiss cheese, divided

Combine the eggs, milk, salt, and pepper in a medium bowl, stirring with a wire whisk.

Heat an 8-inch (20 cm) skillet over medium heat. Coat evenly with 1 teaspoon oil; add half the egg mixture (about ½ cup, or 120 ml) and cook 2 to 3 minutes or until just set (do not stir). Sprinkle half the omelet with half the herbed cheese, half the spinach, half the tomatoes, and half the Swiss cheese. Loosen the omelet with a spatula; fold in half and allow the cheeses to melt. Slide the omelet onto a plate.

Repeat with remaining ingredients.

Buckwheat Crêpes with Bacon & Eggs

Crêpes are a delicate and impressive, yet easy, thin pancake that can be stuffed with both savory and sweet fillings. These hearty crêpes make a perfect on-the-go breakfast.

FOR CRÊPES:
⅓ cup (52 grams) buckwheat flour
¼ cup (30 grams) Kumquat's Gluten-Free All-Purpose Flour Blend (page 15) or other gluten-free all-purpose flour
1 large egg
1½ tablespoons (22 ml) canola oil
½ cup (120 ml) milk or milk alternative
¼ cup (60 ml) water
⅛ teaspoon salt
Oil for skillet

FOR BACON AND EGGS:
5 slices bacon
3 large eggs
2 tablespoons (30 ml) milk or milk alternative
¼ teaspoon salt
⅛ teaspoon black pepper
Shredded Cheddar cheese

To make the crêpes: Combine the buckwheat flour and gluten-free flour in a medium bowl; whisk in the egg, oil, milk, water, and salt.

Heat a 10-inch (25 cm) skillet over medium-high heat; brush pan with oil. Pour scant ¼ cup (60 ml) batter into the skillet and tilt the pan quickly to coat the bottom. Cook the crêpe until golden on the bottom, about 30 seconds. Carefully flip the crêpe with a spatula and cook the other side for an additional 30 seconds. Transfer to a plate, stacking crêpes between waxed paper so they don't stick together. Continue with the remaining batter, brushing skillet with oil between crêpes.

To make the bacon and eggs: Meanwhile, cut bacon with scissors into 1-inch (2.5 cm) pieces directly into another large skillet; cook over medium-high heat until it is crispy, stirring occasionally. While the bacon cooks, combine the eggs, milk, salt, and pepper in a medium bowl; set aside. Remove the bacon from the pan and set aside; pour off all but a teaspoon of bacon drippings.

Lower heat to medium; add the egg mixture to the skillet and cook, without stirring, until mixture begins to set. Draw a spatula across the skillet to form large curds. Continue cooking until eggs are thickened but still moist; do not stir constantly.

Fill the crêpes evenly with the bacon and eggs and sprinkle with shredded Cheddar cheese. Serve immediately.

✷ DID YOU KNOW? ✷

Despite the name, buckwheat contains no wheat or gluten. It is a whole grain that adds a texture, color, and flavor similar to whole wheat when it is used in gluten-free baking. Buckwheat flour is best used when combined with other milder gluten-free flours or a gluten-free all-purpose flour blend.

Blueberry Cornmeal Griddle Cakes

These cakes are a slight, but delightful, departure from traditional pancakes. The cornmeal provides a heartier texture and a delicious flavor, and pairs beautifully with lemon and blueberry. Go the extra mile and serve these with lemon curd—your mouth will thank you.

1 cup (130 grams) gluten-free cornmeal
⅓ cup (47 grams) Kumquat's Gluten-Free All-Purpose Flour Blend (page 15) or gluten-free all-purpose flour
2 tablespoons (26 g) sugar
½ teaspoon baking soda
¼ teaspoon salt
¾ cup (175 ml) buttermilk
2 tablespoons (30 ml) canola oil, plus more for cooking
1 cup (145 g) fresh blueberries
1 teaspoon grated organic lemon zest
Extra blueberries to garnish
Grade B maple syrup or lemon curd

Combine the cornmeal, flour, sugar, baking soda, and salt in a medium bowl. Add the buttermilk and oil and mix well until the batter is thickened. Gently stir in the blueberries and lemon zest.

Heat a griddle or large skillet lightly coated with oil over medium heat. Pour ¼ cup (60 ml) batter onto the griddle and cook about 1½ minutes or until the edges look set and the bottoms are golden. Carefully flip the cakes with a spatula and cook the other side for an additional 1½ minutes, or until done. Serve with extra blueberries and maple syrup or lemon curd.

✳ DID YOU KNOW? ✳

Cornmeal, corn flour, and cornstarch are three distinctively different products. This recipe calls for cornmeal, which is very coarsely ground dried corn, typically used in cornbread recipes. Corn flour is much more finely ground and can be used as an alternative flour in savory dishes. Cornstarch is a fine white powder made from the starchy endosperm of the corn kernel.

Carrot Cake Pancakes with Cream Cheese Frosting

YIELD: 5 SERVINGS, ABOUT 2 PANCAKES EACH

Breakfast has always been my favorite meal of the day. It's probably because no one looks at you crosswise for having a plate full of "cakes" and calling it a meal! But there's no need to feel guilty when it comes to these delicious pancakes, which are packed with a hefty dose of heart-healthy carrots. Packaged pre-shredded carrots are one way to keep the prep time quick and add a slight crunch to the pancakes. If you only want a coconut crunch, however, simply finely chop your carrot shreds or shred your own.

FOR CREAM CHEESE FROSTING:

1⅓ cups (160 g) powdered sugar

4 ounces (113 g) cream cheese, softened

2 tablespoons (30 ml) milk or milk alternative

1 teaspoon vanilla extract

FOR PANCAKES:

1½ cups (220 grams) Kumquat's Gluten-Free All-Purpose Flour Blend (page 15), or other gluten-free all-purpose flour blend

2 teaspoons baking powder

1½ teaspoons (3.5 g) cinnamon

½ teaspoon salt

¾ cup (175 ml) milk or milk alternative

¼ cup (60 g) packed brown sugar

1 teaspoon canola oil, plus more for skillet

2 large eggs

1 teaspoon vanilla extract

1½ cups (165 g) shredded carrots

½ cup (43 g) shredded sweetened coconut

To make the cream cheese frosting: Place the powdered sugar, cream cheese, milk, and vanilla in a medium bowl, stirring with a wire whisk until well combined. Set aside.

To make the pancakes: Combine the flour, baking powder, cinnamon, and salt in a large bowl. In a medium bowl or large measuring cup, combine the milk, brown sugar, oil, eggs, and vanilla. Add the liquid mixture to the flour mixture and stir with a whisk until smooth. Stir in the carrots and coconut.

Spoon the batter in ¼ cup (60 ml) measures onto a hot, greased griddle over medium heat. Turn pancakes with a spatula when the tops begin to bubble and the edges look cooked.

Serve pancakes with Cream Cheese Frosting.

Cinnamon Oatmeal Pancakes with Blackberry Sauce

YIELD: 4 SERVINGS, ABOUT 2 PANCAKES EACH

Bump up the fiber, flavor, and texture of your morning pancakes with a dose of oats. Then add a hint of ground cinnamon and top it off with a slightly sweet sauce of fresh berries . . . . What a comforting plate to greet you in the morning. Do make sure your rolled oats are certified gluten-free, as oats are often processed in facilities that also process wheat.

FOR BLACKBERRY SAUCE:

2 cups (290 g) fresh blackberries
¼ cup (60 ml) water
2 tablespoons (26 g) sugar
1 teaspoon cornstarch
2 teaspoons (10 ml) lemon juice
¼ teaspoon cinnamon

FOR PANCAKES:

1¼ cup (126 grams) gluten-free rolled oats
¾ cup (120 grams) Kumquat's Gluten-Free All-Purpose Flour Blend (page 15) or gluten-free all-purpose flour
2 teaspoons (9 g) baking powder
1½ teaspoons (3.5 g) cinnamon
¼ teaspoon salt
¾ cup (175 ml) milk or milk alternative
½ cup (115 g) packed brown sugar
1 teaspoon canola oil, plus more for griddle
2 large eggs
1 teaspoon vanilla extract
Grade B maple syrup

To make the blackberry sauce: Combine the blackberries, water, sugar, cornstarch, lemon juice, and cinnamon in a small saucepan. Bring to a boil over medium-high heat. Boil 1 minute, reduce heat, and let simmer until the berries burst and the sauce thickens. Set aside.

To make the pancakes: Coarsely grind the oats in a blender or food processor to yield just a bit over 1 cup (126 g) of oat flour. Combine the oat flour, gluten-free flour, baking powder, cinnamon, and salt in a large bowl. Combine the milk, brown sugar, oil, eggs, and vanilla in a medium bowl. Add the liquid mixture to the flour mixture and whisk until smooth.

Spoon ¼ cup (60 ml) batter onto a hot, greased griddle. Turn pancakes when the tops begin to bubble and the edges look cooked.

Serve with Blackberry Sauce and maple syrup.

✳ DID YOU KNOW? ✳

Grade B maple syrup has a much bolder, more intense maple flavor than the Grade A version. Grade B also has twice the amount of calcium and a higher nutrient content in general.

Coconut Skillet Granola with Almonds, Apricots & Dates

YIELD: ABOUT 3 CUPS (366 G)

Granola is temptingly versatile. Whether it is stirred into yogurt, sprinkled on fruit, or just served with milk, it never ceases to please. This one combines some of the best Mediterranean flavors and is prepared the quickest possible way—in the skillet.

1½ cups (127 grams) gluten-free rolled oats
¾ cup (109 g) whole raw almonds
¼ cup (21 g) sweetened shredded coconut
3 tablespoons (24 g) sesame seeds
1 tablespoon (7 g) golden flaxseed meal
¼ cup (85 g) honey
3 tablespoons (45 ml) coconut oil
¼ teaspoon salt
Pinch of cardamom
½ cup (65 g) chopped dried apricots
⅓ cup (59 g) chopped dates

Combine the oats, almonds, coconut, sesame seeds, and flaxseed meal in a medium bowl. Combine the honey, coconut oil, salt, and cardamom in a 12-inch (30 cm) skillet. Heat over medium heat until the coconut oil is warm and melted.

Add the oats mixture to the skillet and coat well with the honey mixture. Cook, stirring frequently, for 5 minutes or until lightly browned. (Be careful not to burn.) Stir in the apricots and dates.

Pour the mixture in a single layer onto a large sheet of parchment to cool.

✳ DID YOU KNOW? ✳

Coconut oil has been called "the healthiest oil on Earth." Even though it is a saturated fat, it is made up of healthy fats. In large part it is made up of lauric acid, which has a laundry list of health benefits. In our family, we cook with it, eat it straight from the jar, and use it on our skin too.

Coconut, Banana & Macadamia Nut Pancakes

YIELD: 5 SERVINGS,
ABOUT 2 PANCAKES EACH

Coconut flour is an amazing addition to any flour arsenal. It is full of true coconut flavor and loaded with fantastic fiber. These pancakes are tender, rich, dense, and packed with a delightful tropical trio of flavors. (Oh, and they freeze well too!)

⅓ cup (53 grams) Kumquat's Gluten-Free All-Purpose Flour Blend (page 15) or gluten-free all-purpose flour
⅓ cup (37 grams) coconut flour
¾ teaspoon baking powder
¼ teaspoon cinnamon
⅛ teaspoon salt
½ cup (113 g) mashed banana
1 tablespoon (13 g) sugar
1 large egg
1¼ cups (295 ml) canned unsweetened coconut milk
1½ tablespoons (22 ml) melted coconut oil
½ teaspoon vanilla extract
¼ cup (34 g) chopped macadamia nuts
¼ cup (21 g) shredded sweetened coconut
Extra banana slices and macadamia nuts to garnish
Grade B maple syrup

Heat a griddle or large skillet over medium heat. Combine the gluten-free flour, coconut flour, baking powder, cinnamon, and salt in a medium bowl. Combine the mashed banana, sugar, egg, coconut milk, coconut oil, and vanilla in another medium bowl. Add the banana mixture to the flour mixture and stir until combined. Stir in the macadamia nuts and shredded coconut. (Batter will be thick.)

Pour ¼ cup (60 ml) batter onto hot, greased griddle, spreading with spatula if necessary, and cook for 3 minutes or until pancakes begin to bubble and edges begin to cook. Carefully flip the cakes with a spatula and cook the other side for an additional 3 minutes or until done; cool slightly.

Top with extra banana slices and macadamia nuts. Serve with maple syrup.

Hot Quinoa Cereal

YIELD: 2 1½-CUP (260 G) SERVINGS

This ancient grain is a delightful and higher protein alternative to your morning oatmeal. Combine it with fresh berries and nutty pecans, and you have a great start to your day.

2 cups (470 ml) water
1 cup (173 g) quinoa
¼ teaspoon salt
¼ cup (59 ml) grade B maple syrup
1 tablespoon (7 g) flaxseed meal
3 tablespoons (45 ml) heavy cream
¼ teaspoon cinnamon
2 cups (290 g) fresh blueberries
1 cup (110 g) chopped pecans, toasted

Combine the water, quinoa, and salt in a medium saucepan. Bring to a boil; reduce heat, cover, and simmer 12 minutes or until almost all the liquid has been absorbed. Stir in the maple syrup, flaxseed meal, cream, and cinnamon.

Divide evenly between 2 bowls. Top each with blueberries and pecans.

Fresh Vegetable Frittata

YIELD: 6 SERVINGS

Frittata is so quick and easy, and is really the perfect morning main dish.

3 tablespoons (42 g) butter
1 cup (95 g) sliced leeks, white and light green parts only
2 cloves garlic, minced
2 cups (268 g) 1-inch (2.5 cm)-sliced asparagus
1 cup (225 ml) grape tomatoes
8 large eggs
¾ cup (75 g) grated Parmesan cheese, divided
2 tablespoons (30 ml) heavy cream
1 teaspoon fresh basil or ½ teaspoon dried basil
1 teaspoon fresh oregano or ½ teaspoon dried
½ teaspoon salt
½ teaspoon black pepper
2 cups (40 g) arugula
1 tablespoon (15 ml) olive oil

Preheat broiler.

Melt the butter in an ovenproof 10-inch (25 cm) skillet over medium-high heat. Add the leeks, garlic, and asparagus; cook for 3 minutes. Add the tomatoes and cook an additional 2 minutes.

Meanwhile, combine the eggs, ½ cup (50 g) Parmesan cheese, cream, basil, oregano, salt, and pepper in a large bowl; stir well with a wire whisk. Add the egg mixture to the skillet and fold gently to combine.

Cook for 3 minutes or until almost set. Sprinkle the top with the remaining Parmesan cheese, but do not stir. Broil until the frittata is puffed and the cheese begins to turn golden, about 2 minutes.

Cut into wedges and top with the arugula. Drizzle the olive oil over arugula and serve.

Huevos Rancheros

This hearty and delicious breakfast dish takes me back to my home state of Texas and all of the Saturday morning brunches I spent with family and friends.

1 can (15 ounces, or 425 g) refried black beans
2 tablespoons (30 ml) milk
Olive oil
6 (5-inch, or 13 cm) corn tortillas
1 can (14.5 ounces, or 410 g) diced tomatoes with chilies
Cooking spray
2 tablespoons (30 g) butter, divided
6 large eggs
½ cup (75 g) crumbled queso fresco
¼ cup (11 g) chopped fresh cilantro
¼ teaspoon salt

Heat the beans and milk in a small saucepan over low heat.

Meanwhile, set oven to the lowest temperature, and place a pan in the oven. Heat a teaspoon of olive oil in a large skillet over medium heat. Heat the tortillas in the hot oil, one at a time, for a minute or so, until tortillas are soft, adding more oil as needed. Place heated tortillas on the pan in the oven to keep warm.

Add the tomatoes to the warm skillet. Bring to a boil, then turn down the heat to a low simmer.

Heat another large skillet over medium-low heat. Add 1 teaspoon (5 g) of butter; add 1 egg and fry. Repeat with remaining eggs.

Spread the beans evenly among 6 tortillas. Top each with an egg and some tomato mixture, then sprinkle evenly with the queso fresco, cilantro, and salt.

Sweet Potato Hash with Ham

This hash is a flavorful, vitamin-packed version of traditional hash and a great way to use any leftover ham and herbs after a holiday meal or any time of year.

4 tablespoons (60 ml) olive oil, divided
2½ cups (275 g) peeled, diced sweet potatoes
2 cloves garlic, minced
3 tablespoons (30 g) minced shallots
2 cups (300 g) diced ham
2 teaspoons (2 g) chopped thyme
2 teaspoons (2 g) chopped sage
Salt and pepper, to taste

Heat 3 tablespoons (45 ml) oil in a large skillet over medium-high heat. Add the sweet potatoes and cook, stirring occasionally, for 10 minutes or until browned on all sides. Add the remaining olive oil, garlic, shallots, and ham; cook an additional 3 minutes. Stir in the thyme, sage, salt, and pepper. Serve immediately.

3

Simple
Starters & Sips

ALTHOUGH I CAN APPRECIATE A HIGH-QUALITY CHEESE PLATE PAIRED WITH SOME TASTY GLUTEN-FREE CRACKERS, I believe starters should be just as easy but carry a little more weight. Hefty plates of nachos or a quick-and-easy snack mix are always a crowd pleaser. Add to it a few delicious drinks to quench your thirst and satisfy your sweet tooth, and you are all set. So whether you're relaxing in front of a game with your friends or needing to provide an after-school snack for the kids, I'm sure these recipes will put lots of smiles on lots of faces, gluten-free or not.

Any-Time Mix

This is so-named because it's not just for a party, not just for a trail, and not just for a snack. It's delicious any time!

8 cups (216 g) Rice Chex cereal
1½ cups (150 g) pecan halves
1½ cups (150 g) walnut halves
1 cup (30 g) gluten-free pretzels, such as Glutino
1 cup (2 sticks, or 225 g) butter
1 cup (225 g) packed brown sugar
¼ teaspoon cayenne pepper
Cooking spray

Preheat oven to 350°F (180°C, or gas mark 4).

Combine the cereal, pecans, walnuts, and pretzels in a large bowl. Set aside. Combine the butter, brown sugar, and cayenne pepper in a medium saucepan. Bring to a boil and boil 1 minute. Remove from heat; pour the mixture over the cereal mixture and stir to combine.

Pour the mix into a very large jelly-roll pan coated with cooking spray. Bake for 8 minutes, stir the mixture, and bake an additional 8 minutes. Cool and store in an airtight container . . . if there's any left over.

Cilantro-Lime Hummus

I've given the ever-popular hummus a little face-lift with the fresh flavors of cilantro and lime, which go hand in hand with corn tortilla chips . . . So there's no need to feel left out of a pita-chip fest around the hummus bowl!

1 can (16 ounces, or 453 g) chickpeas
⅔ cup (10 g) fresh cilantro
1 clove garlic
3 tablespoons (45 ml) fresh lime juice
3 tablespoons (45 g) tahini paste
½ teaspoon salt
¼ teaspoon black pepper
¼ teaspoon ground cumin
⅛ teaspoon cayenne pepper
⅓ cup (75 ml) olive oil

Drain chickpeas, discarding water.

Combine all the ingredients, except the olive oil, in the container of a food processor or blender. With food processor running, slowly pour in the oil through the food chute or feed tube. Purée until smooth. Serve.

Deviled Eggs with Horseradish, Bacon & Cheddar

YIELD: 12 SERVINGS

These eggs were inspired by my husband, who is always a fan of the deviled egg. He would also eat straight horseradish until his nose went up in flames and would happily consume a pound of bacon each morning. Taking moderation into consideration, I've created these little lovelies . . . a delicious twist on an original. For you, honey.

6 hard-boiled large eggs

3 tablespoons (42 g) mayonnaise

1½ tablespoons (22 g) prepared horseradish

1½ teaspoons (6 g) stone-ground Dijon mustard

¼ teaspoon black pepper

3 slices cooked bacon, finely crumbled

2 tablespoons (15 g) finely shredded Cheddar cheese

1 tablespoon (3 g) chopped fresh chives

Additional chopped chives to garnish

Peel the eggs and halve lengthwise. Transfer the yolks to a medium bowl. Place the egg white halves on a tray or serving plate, cavity side up. Add the mayonnaise, horseradish, mustard, and pepper to the egg yolks; mash and stir well to combine.

Stir in the bacon, Cheddar cheese, and tablespoon of chives. Pipe or spoon the yolk mixture back into the cavities of egg whites. Garnish with additional chives, if desired. Serve immediately or chill.

Mango Guacamole

YIELD: 4 SERVINGS

Why all guacamole doesn't include mango, I don't know. They really must be together.
Really.

2 ripe avocadoes
1 cup (175 g) diced mango
¼ cup (40 g) diced red onion
½ clove garlic, minced
½ to 1 jalapeño pepper, seeded and
    minced
2 tablespoons (6 g) chopped fresh
    cilantro
1½ tablespoons (22 ml) fresh
    lime juice
¼ teaspoon salt
¼ teaspoon ground cumin

Cut the avocadoes in half, circling the center pit. Twist the halves to separate and then squeeze each half into a medium bowl. Coarsely mash the avocado flesh with a fork. Stir in the remaining ingredients. Serve immediately or chill, covered.

✳ RECIPE TIP: PRACTICE SAFE MINCING ✳

When mincing the jalapeño pepper, be certain to wear rubber gloves. I also sometimes stick my hand inside of a sandwich bag and use it as a glove to keep the juices from burning my skin.

Nachos Grande

Forget the store-bought chips and make your own! You'll never go back. They are quick and easy, and their freshly toasted corn taste is unequaled. These comforting and filling nachos are a great starter or a whole meal.

8 (6-inch, or 15 cm) corn tortillas, quartered
Cooking spray
1½ teaspoon cumin, divided
¼ teaspoon salt
¾ pound (340 g) ground beef
1 tablespoon (7.5 g) chili powder
1 teaspoon dried oregano
½ teaspoon garlic salt
1 can (15 ounces, or 425 g) refried black beans
3 cups (340 g) shredded Cheddar cheese
Salsa, for serving
Sour Cream, for serving
Chopped fresh cilantro, for serving
Sliced jalapeño peppers, for serving

Preheat oven to 425°F (220°C, or gas mark 7).

Arrange the tortilla wedges in a single layer on a large baking sheet coated with cooking spray. Generously coat the tortilla wedges with cooking spray and sprinkle with ½ teaspoon cumin and salt. Bake for 8 to 10 minutes or until crisp.

Meanwhile, cook the ground beef in a large skillet over medium-high heat, stirring occasionally, until brown; drain, if necessary. Stir in the chili powder, 1 teaspoon cumin, oregano, and garlic salt.

Meanwhile, heat the refried beans in another large skillet, coated with cooking spray, until warm.

Preheat broiler. Place tortilla chips on a large oven-safe platter or baking sheet. Spread the warm beans over each chip and spoon the meat mixture over top of the beans; top evenly with the cheese. Broil for 1 minute or until the cheese melts.

Remove from the oven; top with salsa, sour cream, cilantro, and jalapeños. Serve immediately.

✸ RECIPE TIP: SPRAY SAFE ✸

When buying aerosol vegetable cooking sprays, be sure to avoid buying "baking" spray, which contains wheat flour and is not gluten-free.

Aloe Lemonade

YIELD: 2 (12-OUNCE, OR 355 ML) SERVINGS

Nothing is more refreshing than lemonade . . . sweet and tart and fresh and cool. And who doesn't love the sweet memories of childhood lemonade stands, waving and hoping neighbors will stop and pay a quarter for a Dixie cup–full to quench their thirsts? The benefits of aloe and lemon juices are amazing and impressive. In this lemonade, their tartness is curbed by calorie-free stevia, adding the perfect amount of sweetness.

½ cup (120 ml) freshly squeezed
   organic lemon juice
½ cup (120 ml) aloe vera juice
2 cups (470 ml) water
20 drops liquid stevia

Combine all the ingredients in a pitcher and stir well. Serve over ice.

✴ DID YOU KNOW? ✴

We've all heard of putting aloe vera juice on burns, but it is also incredibly helpful in soothing and healing the gut. When ingested, the juice coats the intestinal walls and helps decrease inflammation. It can be very beneficial to those people with ulcers, Crohn's disease, celiac disease, irritable bowel syndrome, and gluten sensitivity.

Sweet Cherry Lemonade

YIELD: ABOUT 5 CUPS (1.2 L)

As much as I love sweet treats, I hesitate to guzzle sugary beverages. This drink is the perfect mix of real sweet cherries and tart lemonade . . . and it is rounded off instead by agave nectar, which has a lower glycemic index than sugar and won't cause an unwanted blood sugar spike. It's a refreshing treat everyone can enjoy on a hot summer's day by the pool, on a picnic, or after working hard in your garden.

2 cups (about 1 pound) fresh cherries, pitted
⅔ cup (167 g) agave nectar
1 cup (235 ml) fresh lemon juice
2½ cups (590 ml) cold water
Lemon slices for garnish

Combine the cherries, agave nectar, and lemon juice in the container of a blender; purée the mixture. Strain the mixture through a fine sieve into a pitcher, pressing on the cherries to release juices; discard puréed cherry bits. Add the water to the pitcher; stir to combine. Serve over ice with additional lemon slices.

✸ RECIPE TIP: THE PITS ✸

If you don't own a cherry-pitting gadget, use a metal pastry tip. After removing the stem, press the stem side of the cherry onto the pastry tip. The pit should pop right out the other side.

Coconut-Almond Hot Chocolate

YIELD: 2 GENEROUS (ABOUT 1-CUP, OR 235 ML) SERVINGS

This ultimate, thick, rich, heart-warming hot chocolate is made with delicious coconut milk (but feel free to substitute with whatever you please) and is sweetened with natural agave nectar to save blood sugars from unhealthy spikes and falls. So wrap your cold hands around a warm mug of this heavenly stuff and escape the chill.

1 can (13.5 ounces, or 398 ml) unsweetened coconut milk
2 tablespoons (28 g) cocoa powder
2 tablespoons (28 g) agave nectar
2 ounces (57 g) bittersweet chocolate, finely chopped
¼ teaspoon almond extract
Pinch of salt
Toasted coconut or marshmallows, for garnish

Combine the coconut milk, cocoa powder, agave nectar, and chocolate in a medium saucepan. Over medium-high heat, heat the mixture to almost boiling, stirring occasionally with a wire whisk. Remove from heat. Add the almond extract and salt; stir well with a wire whisk. Serve immediately, topping each serving with toasted coconut or marshmallows.

Hot Citrus-Mulled Cider

YIELD: 6 (1-CUP, OR 235 ML) SERVINGS

Nothing screams warm comfort in a beverage during the fall and winter like this drink. The smells alone fill your nose and your home with cozy wafts of happiness. This cider has a strong hint of citrus, fresh and soothing, in addition to the classic mulling spices.

1 jug (1½ quarts, or 1.4 L) apple cider
3 sticks (3 inches, or 7.5 cm) cinnamon
10 whole cloves
5 whole allspice berries
5 cardamom pods, crushed
1 organic orange, sliced
1 organic lemon, sliced
1 piece (2 inches, or 5 cm) fresh ginger, peeled and thickly sliced

Combine all the ingredients in a large saucepan. Bring to a boil; reduce heat and simmer for 15 minutes. Strain, if desired. Serve hot.

Fast & Filling Full-Plate Meals

➤ **AH, THE ETERNAL QUESTION: "WHAT'S FOR DINNER?"**
We all face it every evening. Add to the equation busy schedules, kids to shuffle, and chores to complete and it all makes you want to scream. But never fear. This incredible chapter includes a month-full of flavorful, fuss-free answers to the dinner question, including many classic comfort foods—the ones we loved before gluten was off our tables. Quick, easy, and simple favorites, like Green Chicken Enchiladas (page 62), Spaghetti and Meatballs (page 85) , are just as flavorful and gratifying, but now gluten-free. Others are for the nights you want to try something new. Bon appétit!

Chicken Marsala

Marsala is sweet Italian wine that translates beautifully in savory dishes like this classic. An impressive but easy dinner, this one is sure to make the weekly rotation and the dinner guest menu! Serve this classic dish with buttered pasta or mashed potatoes to soak up the rich, precious sauce.

2 tablespoons (30 ml) olive oil, divided

4 (4-ounce, or 115 g) chicken breast cutlets

¾ teaspoon salt, divided

½ teaspoon black pepper, divided

4 tablespoons (32 g) Kumquat's Gluten-Free All-Purpose Flour Blend (page 15) or gluten-free all-purpose flour, divided

⅓ cup (53 g) chopped shallots

10 ounces (284 g) sliced shiitake mushrooms

2 teaspoons (1.7 g) chopped fresh sage

⅔ cup (160 ml) gluten-free chicken broth

⅓ cup (80 ml) Marsala wine

⅓ cup (80 ml) heavy cream

1 tablespoon (14 g) butter

Preheat oven to 400°F (200°C, or gas mark 6).

Heat 1 tablespoon (15 ml) olive oil in a large ovenproof skillet over medium-high heat. Sprinkle the chicken breast cutlets with ¼ teaspoon salt and ¼ teaspoon pepper; dredge the cutlets in 3 tablespoons (24 g) flour. Cook the chicken in hot oil for 3 minutes on each side or until just browned. Remove from skillet and keep warm.

Add the remaining olive oil to the skillet to heat. Add the shallots, mushrooms, sage, remaining salt, and ¼ teaspoon pepper to the pan. Cook for 1 minute or until the mushrooms begin to soften. Sprinkle the mixture evenly with the remaining flour, stir, and cook for 1 minute. Stir in the chicken broth and wine, scraping browned bits from the bottom of the pan. Stir in the cream and butter.

Return the chicken to the pan. Place the skillet in the oven and bake for 5 minutes or until chicken is done.

> ✳ RECIPE TIP: MAKE YOUR
> OWN CUTLETS ✳
>
> If you cannot find prepared chicken cutlets, place chicken breasts in a large zip-top plastic bag and pound with a rolling pin or meat mallet to ¼-inch (6 mm) thickness.

Chicken Pot Pie

Every house—even a gluten-free one—needs a good, comforting recipe for a chicken pot pie. This one is quick, easy, simple, and delicious. The crust is cooked separately to speed up the prep. If you have a little extra time, place the unbaked crust on top of the chicken mixture–filled casserole dish and bake on the dish, the traditional way. Either way, your tummy will be happy.

¼ recipe Pâte Brisée (page 122) or prepared gluten-free pie crust

1 large egg, lightly beaten

2 tablespoons (28 g) butter

1 cup (160 g) chopped onion

½ cup (50 g) chopped celery

2 cups (260 g) frozen peas and carrots mix or frozen vegetable medley

⅓ cup (47 grams) Kumquat's Gluten-Free All-Purpose Flour Blend (page 15) or gluten-free all-purpose flour

2 cups (470 ml) gluten-free chicken broth

1 cup (235 ml) heavy cream

3 cups (420 g) chopped cooked chicken

1 teaspoon salt

¾ teaspoon dried thyme

½ teaspoon black pepper

½ teaspoon garlic powder

Preheat oven to 400°F (200°C, or gas mark 6).

Roll the pastry crust out to 8-inch (20 cm) round. Place on a parchment-lined baking sheet, brush with the egg, and bake for 14 minutes or until browned.

Meanwhile, melt the butter in a large skillet over medium-high heat. Add the onion and celery and cook 2 minutes. Add the peas and carrots and cook 2 minutes more. Sprinkle the mixture evenly with the flour and cook for 1 minute, stirring occasionally. Add the broth and cream; stir well, scraping the bottom of the pan with a wooden spatula. Stir in the chicken, salt, thyme, pepper, and garlic powder. Bring to a boil, reduce heat, and cook until thickened.

Pour the chicken mixture into a 1½-quart (1.4 L) round casserole dish. Top with the crust. Serve immediately.

Chicken Saltimbocca

The Italian translation of this dish is "jumps in the mouth" because the flavors are so delicious they dance on your tongue. It's also simple and quick, but exceedingly elegant. Serve this flavorful chicken with hot, buttered gluten-free noodles and a cool glass of white wine.

4 (4-ounce, or 115 g) chicken cutlets
¼ teaspoon salt
¼ teaspoon black pepper
12 sage leaves
4 thin slices prosciutto, halved lengthwise
1 tablespoon (14 g) butter
1 tablespoon (15 ml) olive oil
½ cup (120 ml) gluten-free chicken broth
½ teaspoon cornstarch
¼ cup (60 ml) white wine

Sprinkle the chicken cutlets evenly with salt and pepper. Top each cutlet with 3 sage leaves and wrap each with 2 strips of prosciutto. Heat the butter and olive oil in a large skillet over medium-high heat. Add the chicken to the skillet and cook for 2 to 3 minutes on each side, or until done.

Meanwhile, combine the chicken broth and cornstarch in a small bowl; set aside. Remove the chicken from the skillet and keep warm.

Add the wine to the skillet and scrape browned bits from the bottom of the pan. Add the chicken broth mixture to the pan, and cook for 2 minutes, or until the sauce thickens.

Spoon the sauce over the chicken and serve.

✳ RECIPE TIP: MAKE YOUR OWN CUTLETS ✳

If you cannot find prepared chicken cutlets, place chicken breasts in a large zip-top plastic bag and pound with a rolling pin or meat mallet to ¼-inch (6 mm) thickness.

Chicken Stir-Fry

If you're like me, one of the things I miss since going gluten-free is good Asian cuisine. This stir-fry is sure to hit the spot and convince you that you're not missing a thing. It's also a great way to use extra vegetables from your crisper. Feel free to add your favorites to make this just the way you want it.

1 cup (130 g) ½-inch (12 mm) sliced, peeled carrots

1 cup (71 g) broccoli florets

1 cup (70 g) quartered mushrooms

1 cup (75 g) halved sugar snap peas

1 cup (100 g) ½-inch (13 mm) sliced celery

1 cup (100 g) ½-inch (13 mm) sliced scallions

2 cloves garlic, minced

1 tablespoon (6 g) peeled and minced fresh ginger

3 tablespoons (45 ml) olive oil, divided

1 pound (455 g) chicken cutlets, cut into 1-inch (2.5 cm) pieces

1 cup (235 ml) gluten-free chicken broth

⅓ cup (80 ml) gluten-free tamari soy sauce

¼ cup (60 ml) mirin

2 tablespoons (26 g) sugar

1 tablespoon (8 g) cornstarch

1 teaspoon sesame oil

½ teaspoon red pepper flakes

2 teaspoons (5 g) toasted sesame seeds

3 cups (585 g) hot, cooked brown rice

Combine the carrots, broccoli, mushrooms, sugar snap peas, celery, scallions, garlic, and ginger in a large bowl.

Heat 1 tablespoon (15 ml) olive oil in a large skillet or wok over medium-high to high heat until hot. Add the chicken and cook, stirring occasionally, for 5 minutes or until browned.

Meanwhile, combine the broth, tamari soy sauce, mirin, sugar, cornstarch, sesame oil, and red pepper flakes in a medium bowl or measuring cup.

Remove the chicken from the skillet; place in a large bowl and keep warm.

Add 1 tablespoon (15 ml) olive oil to the skillet or wok. Add half the vegetable mixture to the skillet; cook for 2 minutes or until vegetables are just tender. Add the mixture to the bowl of chicken. Add remaining olive oil to the skillet; cook remaining vegetables for 2 minutes. Return chicken and cooked vegetables to the pan.

Stir in the soy sauce mixture and cook for 3 minutes or until sauce is thickened. Stir in the toasted sesame seeds. Serve with brown rice.

✳ DID YOU KNOW? ✳

Gluten-free tamari soy sauce is made with 100 percent whole soybeans and no wheat. It is richer in color and flavor than regular shoyu soy sauce and is a perfect gluten-free alternative to shoyu.

Chinese Lemon Chicken

For all those times you've driven passed the Chinese food restaurant, knowing one bite of the gluten-filled food inside would result in illness, here is a keeper! It's sweet, sticky chicken with a spicy, tangy lemon sauce. Holy yum . . . really, you must.

1 cup (235 ml) canola oil

½ cup (65 g) plus 1 teaspoon (3 g) cornstarch, divided

2 pounds (905 g) chicken breasts, cut into 2-inch (5 cm) pieces

½ cup (120 ml) gluten-free chicken broth

2 teaspoons (4 g) fresh lemon zest

5 tablespoons (75 ml) fresh lemon juice

1 tablespoon (15 ml) gluten-free tamari soy sauce

3 tablespoons (45 g) packed brown sugar

1 teaspoon sesame oil

1 teaspoon salt

¼ to ½ teaspoon crushed red pepper flakes

¼ cup (25 g) chopped scallions

2 cloves garlic, minced

1 teaspoon peeled and chopped fresh ginger

1 tablespoon (8 g) sesame seeds

Heat the oil over medium-high heat in a large skillet. Meanwhile, place ½ cup (65 g) cornstarch in a gallon-size (3.7 L) resealable plastic bag. Add the chicken pieces to the bag and shake well to coat. Add the coated chicken to the hot oil and cook for 3 minutes on each side or until browned and cooked through. Cook in two batches, if necessary. Remove to a paper towel to drain.

Meanwhile, combine the remaining cornstarch, broth, lemon zest, lemon juice, tamari, brown sugar, sesame oil, salt, and red pepper flakes in a medium bowl.

Pour off all but 1 teaspoon of remaining oil from the pan and discard. Add the scallions, garlic, and ginger to the skillet; cook for 30 seconds. Add the broth mixture, scraping browned bits from the bottom of the pan. Bring to a boil, reduce heat, and simmer 1 minute or until thickened. Remove the pan from the heat; stir the chicken into the sauce. Sprinkle with the sesame seeds. Serve immediately.

✷ FAST & SIMPLE SUGGESTION ✷

The French term *mise en place* translates to "everything in place" and refers to organizing all ingredients and equipment needed before beginning to cook. While it requires a little time up front, it makes the actual cooking fly by.

Classic Crab Cakes

Gluten-free bread crumbs put this iconic seafood entree back on your list of "yes" foods. The slightly crunchy coating and delicate crab insides of these cakes are distinctively light and refreshing . . . one of my favorites, for sure!

2 tablespoons (12 g) chopped scallions
2 tablespoons (6 g) chopped parsley
¼ teaspoon paprika
¼ teaspoon salt
⅛ teaspoon cayenne pepper
3 tablespoons (42 g) mayonnaise
1 tablespoon (11 g) Dijon mustard
1 teaspoon fresh lemon juice
1 large egg
1 pound (455 g) lump crabmeat, drained and shell pieces removed
1¼ cup (145 g) gluten-free bread crumbs, such as Glutino, divided
½ cup (120 ml) olive oil, divided
Lemon slices, for serving

Combine the scallions, parsley, paprika, salt, cayenne pepper, mayonnaise, mustard, lemon juice, and egg in a medium bowl. Stir in the crabmeat and ½ cup (60 g) bread crumbs. Shape the mixture into 8 equal patties. Dredge the patties in the remaining bread crumbs.

Heat ¼ cup (60 ml) oil over medium-high heat in a large skillet. Add 4 crab cakes to the pan; cook for 3 minutes on each side or until browned. Remove from pan and keep warm. Repeat with the remaining oil and crab cakes. Serve with lemon slices.

Cumin-Turkey Burgers

YIELD: 4 SERVINGS

If you fear turkey burgers equal dry hockey pucks, then here's your answer. These burgers are mouthwateringly moist and full of the best Southwest flavors. If you want to hit the highest note, serve them with the Mango Guacamole on page 38.

1 pound (455 g) ground turkey
2 cloves garlic, minced
1 tablespoon (7 g) ground cumin
½ teaspoon chili powder
½ jalapeño pepper, seeded and minced
3 tablespoons (8 g) chopped cilantro
1 teaspoon salt
½ teaspoon black pepper
4 slices Pepper-Jack cheese
4 gluten-free hamburger buns
Avocado slices, for serving
Tomato slices, for serving

Preheat grill. Combine the turkey, garlic, cumin, chili powder, jalapeño, cilantro, salt, and pepper in a medium bowl. Divide the mixture into four equal portions. Form each portion into a ¾-inch (1.9 cm)-thick patty. Make a small indentation in the middle of each burger.

Grill burgers 5 minutes; flip, and grill for an additional 4 minutes, or until almost cooked through. Top each burger with a slice of cheese and grill an additional 1 minute, or until the cheese is melted and the burger is cooked through.

Place a burger on the bottoms of each hamburger bun. Top with avocado, tomato, additional desired dressings, and the top of the bun.

Grilled Cheese & Turkey Sandwiches

YIELD: 4 SERVINGS

A good grilled cheese sandwich is an all-time favorite. In this one, I've combined some of my favorite flavors of fall, including apple butter and sage.

8 slices gluten-free sandwich bread
   (such as Udi's or Whole Foods)
½ cup (125 g) apple butter, divided
8 ounces (227 g) Brie, sliced, divided
8 slices deli turkey, divided
1 teaspoon chopped fresh sage, divided
8 teaspoons (37 g) butter, divided

Spread one side of each slice of bread with 1 tablespoon (15 g) apple butter. Top four slices of bread evenly with Brie, turkey, and sage. Top each with remaining slices of bread.

Heat a large skillet or griddle over medium-high heat. Turn heat down to medium and melt 1 teaspoon butter. Add two sandwiches and cook 1 to 2 minutes until browned. Add an additional 1 teaspoon butter and flip sandwiches; cook 1 to 2 additional minutes. Repeat with remaining sandwiches. Serve immediately.

Eggplant Parmesan

This dish is homemade vegetarian Italian at its finest—and easiest. Serve with buttered gluten-free noodles and a glass of wine—and candlelight.

1 jar (25 ounces, or 709 g) gluten-free tomato-basil pasta sauce

1 (1¼-pound, or 570 g) eggplant, unpeeled and sliced into ½-inch rounds

1 teaspoon salt

2 large eggs

½ teaspoon cornstarch

1 cup (115 g) gluten-free bread crumbs, such as Glutino

⅓ cup (27 g) shredded Parmesan cheese

½ teaspoon garlic powder

½ teaspoon dried oregano

½ cup (120 ml) olive oil, divided

Cooking spray

2 cups (230 g) shredded mozzarella cheese

Chopped parsley, for garnish

Pour the pasta sauce into a medium saucepan and bring to a boil; reduce heat and simmer.

Sprinkle the eggplant slices with salt. Combine the eggs and cornstarch in a shallow dish. Combine the bread crumbs, Parmesan cheese, garlic powder, and oregano in another shallow dish. Dredge the eggplant slices in the egg mixture and then dredge in the bread crumb mixture; set aside.

Preheat broiler. Heat ¼ cup (60 ml) olive oil in a large skillet. Add as many eggplant rounds as will fit well into the skillet. Cook for 2 minutes on each side or until breading is browned. Place browned rounds, overlapping a bit if necessary, into a 13 × 9-inch (33 × 23 cm) baking dish coated with cooking spray. Continue with remaining oil and eggplant rounds.

Once all eggplant rounds are in the dish, pour the warmed pasta sauce evenly over the top. Sprinkle with the mozzarella cheese. Broil for 1 minute or until the cheese is melted and bubbly. Garnish with chopped parsley.

Frogmore Stew

This Southern coastal one-pot seafood dinner is also known as a "Low Country Boil." This is true comfort food and is as easy as boiling water. Serve with lemons, cocktail sauce, and lots of friends.

4 quarts (3.7 L) water

1 bottle (12 ounces, or 355 ml) gluten-free beer

¼ cup (113 g) Old Bay seasoning

4 cloves garlic, crushed

2 bay leaves

2 pounds (905 g) red potatoes, quartered

2 pounds (905 g) gluten-free kielbasa, cut into 3-inch (7.5 cm) pieces

4 ears corn, shucked and cut into thirds

2 pounds (905 g) large shrimp, unpeeled

Bring the water, beer, Old Bay, garlic, and bay leaves to a boil in a large stockpot or Dutch oven. Add the red potatoes and sausage; cook for 8 minutes. Add the corn and cook for 3 minutes. Add the shrimp and cook for 2 minutes or until done. Drain and discard bay leaves before serving.

✹ RECIPE TIP ✹

Did you know that most beers are made with barley or wheat, which takes them off the table for those of us avoiding gluten? Luckily, there are many good beers that are gluten-free and made with safe grains such as millet, rice, sorghum, buckwheat, and corn. Be sure to check labels when picking out your brews and make sure they too are gluten-free.

Green Chicken Enchiladas

These enchiladas are true Tex-Mex, which means straight from the heart of this Texas girl. They've been served countless times on my dinner table to friends and family. It's always a hit, always a little bite of Texas!

½ cup (80 g) chopped onion
1 clove garlic, minced
2 teaspoons (10 ml) olive oil
1 package (10 ounces, or 283 g) frozen spinach, thawed and drained
1 can (4 ounces, or 113 g) chopped green chilies
½ teaspoon cumin
½ teaspoon salt
¼ teaspoon black pepper
1 container (8 ounces, or 227 g) sour cream
4 ounces (115 g) cream cheese
⅓ cup (87 g) salsa
½ cup (120 ml) gluten-free chicken broth
2 cups (280 g) chopped cooked chicken
Cooking spray
12 (6-inch, or 15 cm) corn tortillas, warmed
2 cups (230 g) shredded Monterey Jack cheese
Salsa, for serving

Cook the onion and garlic in the oil over medium-high heat in a large skillet for 3 minutes. Add the spinach, chilies, cumin, salt, pepper, sour cream, cream cheese, salsa, and chicken broth. Bring to a simmer.

Place the chicken in a medium bowl. Pour half the spinach mixture over the chicken and stir to combine.

Preheat broiler. Spread 2 tablespoons (30 ml) remaining spinach sauce in the bottom of a 13 × 9-inch (33 × 23 cm) baking dish coated with cooking spray. Dip a tortilla in remaining spinach sauce on both sides to soften. Fill the tortilla with 2 tablespoons (18 g) chicken mixture and roll up. Repeat with remaining tortillas and filling. Arrange the filled tortillas on top of the spinach sauce in the baking dish. Pour any remaining spinach sauce over the enchiladas. Sprinkle evenly with the shredded cheese. Place under broiler and cook for 1 minute or until the cheese is melted and just beginning to brown. Serve with additional salsa, if desired.

Turkey Picadillo

This flavorful and comforting Cuban dish is traditionally made with beef, which I've replaced with leaner turkey. I promise you'll never miss the extra fat!

1 cup (160 g) chopped onion
2 cloves garlic, minced
2 teaspoons (10 ml) olive oil
1 pound (455 g) ground turkey
1 can (14.5 ounces, or 410 g) diced tomatoes, undrained
½ jalapeño pepper, seeded and minced
½ cup (50 g) chopped pimiento-stuffed green olives
⅓ cup (50 g) golden raisins
⅓ cup (37 g) slivered almonds, toasted
2 teaspoons (5 g) chili powder
1 teaspoon ground cumin
1 teaspoon salt
½ teaspoon dried oregano
¼ teaspoon cinnamon
¼ teaspoon black pepper

Cook the onion and garlic in olive oil a large skillet over medium-high heat for 3 minutes. Add the turkey and cook until browned. Stir in the tomatoes, jalapeño, olives, raisins, almonds, chili powder, cumin, salt, oregano, cinnamon, and pepper; simmer for 3 minutes. Serve immediately, with Handmade Corn Tortillas (on page 114), or Honey Skillet Cornbread (on page 118), if you like.

✳ RECIPE TIP: PRACTICE SAFE MINCING ✳

When mincing the jalapeño pepper, be sure to wear rubber gloves. I sometimes stick my hand inside a sandwich bag, using it like a glove, to keep the juices from burning my skin.

Grilled Ribeye with Orange-Balsamic Glaze

YIELD: 4 SERVINGS

This recipe is proof that with just a few simple ingredients you can prepare a steak dinner your friends and family will rave about. Balsamic vinegar and orange pair beautifully and reduce to a delicious, tangy, barely sweet, gluten-free glaze. Serve with Garlic, Herb & Bacon Mashed Potatoes on page 108 to round out the meal and soak up every bit of glaze.

1½ pounds (680 g) ribeye steak
½ teaspoon salt
¼ teaspoon black pepper
1/2 cup (120 ml) balsamic vinegar
¼ cup (40 g) minced shallots
2 tablespoons (30 ml) orange juice
1 tablespoon (14 g) butter
1 teaspoon organic orange zest

Preheat grill.

Sprinkle the steak evenly with salt and pepper. Grill the steak 4 minutes on each side or to desired degree of doneness. Let rest for 5 minutes.

Meanwhile, combine the balsamic vinegar, shallots, orange juice, butter, and orange zest in a small saucepan. Bring to a boil; boil for 5 to 6 minutes or until reduced to ¼ cup (60 ml).

Slice the steak against the grain into ¼-inch (6 mm)-thick slices. Serve, drizzled with sauce.

Grouper Piccata

Because capers, lemon, and white wine go hand-in-hand with fish, this seafood version of piccata is a no-brainer. Light, fresh, and delightful . . .

4 (6-ounce, or 168 g) grouper fillets
¼ teaspoon salt
¼ teaspoon black pepper
¼ cup (35 grams) Kumquat's Gluten-Free All-Purpose Flour Blend (page 15) or gluten-free all-purpose flour
2 tablespoons (28 g) butter
1 tablespoon (15 ml) olive oil
½ cup (120 ml) fresh lemon juice
¼ cup (60 ml) white wine
1 tablespoon (14 g) butter
3 tablespoons (26 g) capers
3 tablespoons (8 g) chopped parsley

Sprinkle the grouper fillets with salt and pepper and then dredge on all sides in the flour. Melt the 2 tablespoons (28 g) butter and olive oil in a large skillet over medium-high heat. Add the fillets to the skillet and cook until browned and cooked through, about 5 minutes on each side. Remove fish from skillet.

Add the lemon juice and wine to the skillet, scraping browned bits from the pan. Cook for 2 minutes or until slightly thickened. Remove from heat. Stir in the remaining butter, capers, and parsley. Serve sauce over fish.

Spicy Mongolian Beef

YIELD: 4 SERVINGS

Welcome back to one of my all-time favorite Asian dishes. Tender meat, fresh scallions, and a tangy, spicy sauce . . . it's easy, enticing, and impressive.

1 tablespoon (15 ml) olive oil
1 pound (455 g) flank steak, cut into ¼-inch slices against the grain
3 tablespoons (45 ml) gluten-free tamari soy sauce
1 teaspoon sugar
1 teaspoon cornstarch
1 tablespoon (16 g) gluten-free hoisin sauce
1 teaspoon rice wine vinegar
1 teaspoon sesame oil
½ teaspoon red pepper flakes
3 cloves garlic, minced
1 tablespoon (6 g) peeled and minced fresh ginger
8 scallions, cut into 2-inch (5 cm) pieces
4 cups (780 g) cooked brown rice

Heat the olive oil in a large skillet over medium-high heat until hot. Add the beef and cook, stirring occasionally, for 4 minutes or until browned.

Meanwhile, combine the soy sauce, sugar, cornstarch, hoisin sauce, rice wine vinegar, sesame oil, and red pepper flakes in a small bowl or measuring cup; stir well to dissolve the cornstarch.

Add the garlic and ginger to the pan with the beef; cook for 1 minute. Add the scallions and cook for an additional 30 seconds. Stir in the soy sauce mixture and cook for 1 minute, or until the sauce is thickened and coats the beef. Serve with brown rice.

✳ DID YOU KNOW? ✳

Tamari gluten-free soy sauce is made with 100 percent whole soybeans and no wheat. It is richer in color and flavor than regular shoyu soy sauce and is a perfect gluten-free alternative to shoyu. Gluten-free hoisin sauce is made with tamari soy sauce.

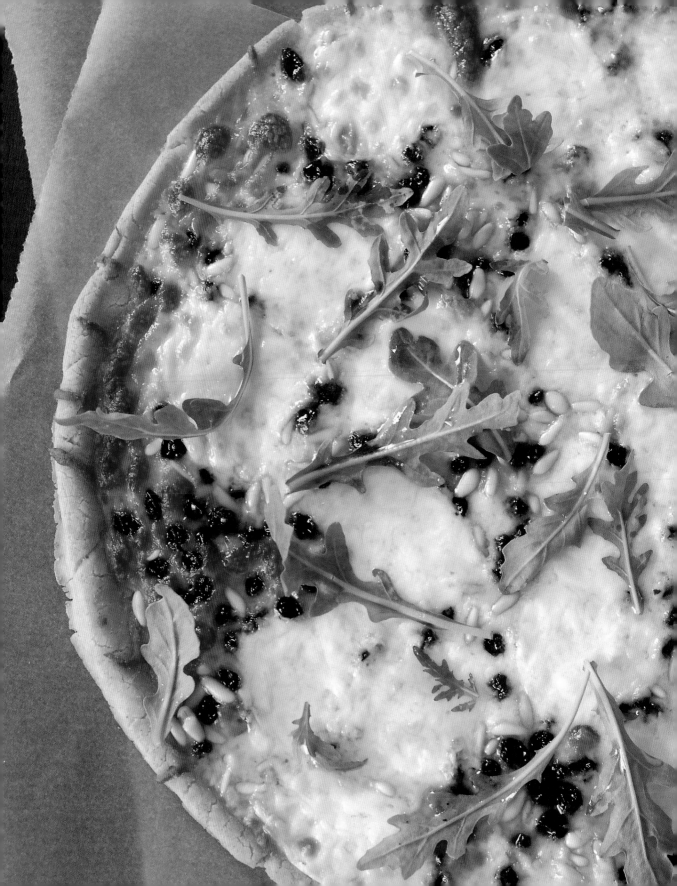

Mozzarella Pizza with Pine Nuts, Currants & Arugula

You must try this pizza. Really. You must. The sweet chewiness of the currants, the salty cheesy mozzarella, the crunchy perfect pine nuts, and the peppery arugula . . . and finally a touch of the tart lemon oil . . . it's amazing.

1 recipe Kumquat's Pizza Dough (page 141) or prepared gluten-free pizza dough, rolled out and unbaked
Olive oil for brushing
½ teaspoon garlic powder
2 cups (230 g) shredded mozzarella cheese
8 ounces (227 g) mozzarella cheese balls (ciliegine)
¼ cup (35 g) pine nuts, toasted
¼ cup (38 g) currants
2 tablespoons (30 ml) olive oil
1 teaspoon fresh lemon zest
¼ teaspoon minced garlic
½ cup (10 g) arugula, for garnish

Preheat oven to 450°F (230°C, or gas mark 8).

Place the pizza dough on a baking sheet or pizza stone. Brush evenly with olive oil and sprinkle evenly with the garlic powder. Sprinkle evenly with the shredded mozzarella cheese and mozzarella cheese balls. Top evenly with the pine nuts and currants. Bake for 16 minutes or until the cheese is melted and crust is golden.

Meanwhile, combine the olive oil, lemon zest, and garlic in a small skillet or saucepan. Heat the mixture over medium-low heat for 5 minutes. Turn off heat and let sit for 5 minutes. Strain mixture, discarding lemon zest and garlic.

Drizzle the baked pizza evenly with the infused oil and sprinkle the arugula over top of the pizza. Cut into slices.

> ✳ RECIPE TIP: TOAST PINE NUTS TO PERFECTION ✳
>
> To toast pine nuts, bake them at 350°F (180°C, or gas mark 4) for 6 to 8 minutes. Or cook them in a skillet for 1 to 2 minutes or until fragrant and just browned.

Barbecue Chicken Pizza

It's a happy day when pizza is no longer off limits. This chicken-topped version, complete with spicy barbecue sauce and fresh cilantro, has always been a favorite of mine. Ahh ... welcome back, delicious friend.

1¼ cups (350 g) gluten-free barbecue sauce, divided

2 cups (280 g) chopped, cooked chicken

1 recipe Kumquat's Pizza Dough (page 141) or gluten-free pizza dough, rolled out and unbaked

Olive oil for brushing

½ teaspoon garlic powder

2 cups (230 g) shredded Monterey Jack cheese, divided

⅓ cup (55 g) thinly sliced red onion

4 slices bacon, cooked and crumbled

⅓ cup (15 g) chopped cilantro

¼ cup (25 g) chopped scallions

Preheat oven to 450°F (230°C, or gas mark 8).

Combine ½ cup (125 g) barbecue sauce and the chicken in medium bowl; stir to coat.

Place the pizza dough on a baking sheet or pizza stone. Brush evenly with the olive oil and sprinkle with the garlic powder. Spread the remaining barbecue sauce evenly over the rolled out pizza crust. Top evenly with half the Monterey Jack cheese. Top with the red onion, bacon, and chicken mixture. Sprinkle the remaining cheese evenly over pizza.

Bake for 16 minutes or until the cheese is melted and the crust is cooked. Top with the cilantro and scallions. Cut into slices.

Pan-Seared Tilapia with Citrus & Tomatoes

YIELD: 4 SERVINGS

Fresh citrus and tomatoes make a fresh and tasty topping for this mild white fish. Take advantage of ripe, in-season produce for a perfect summer meal!

1 teaspoon salt, divided
½ teaspoon black pepper, divided
4 (6-ounce, or 168 g) tilapia fillets
1 tablespoon (15 ml) plus 2 teaspoons (10 ml) olive oil, divided
1 cup (180 g) diced tomatoes
½ cup (80 g) diced red onion
2 teaspoons (4 g) organic lemon zest
2 teaspoons (4 g) organic orange zest
2 tablespoons (30 ml) fresh lemon juice
2 tablespoons (30 ml) fresh orange juice
1 clove garlic, minced
⅓ cup (75 ml) white wine

Sprinkle ½ teaspoon salt and ¼ teaspoon pepper evenly over the tilapia fillets. Heat 1 tablespoon (15 ml) olive oil in a large skillet over medium-high heat; add the tilapia fillets and cook for 4 minutes on each side. Meanwhile, combine the tomatoes, red onion, zests, juices, garlic, remaining olive oil, remaining salt, and remaining pepper in a medium bowl; set aside.

Remove the tilapia from the pan and keep warm. Add the white wine to the pan and scrape browned bits from the bottom of the pan. Add the tomato mixture and cook, stirring occasionally, for 2 minutes. Spoon the mixture over the tilapia and serve immediately.

> ✳ RECIPE TIP: ZEST FIRST ✳
>
> When you are using both citrus rinds and juices, grate the zest first and then squeeze the juice.

Pecan-Crusted Chicken Tenders

YIELD: 4 SERVINGS

Here's the ultimate kid-friendly meal made adult-friendly too! With just a few of the right spices and some crunchy pecans, these tenders will make the whole family happy—a definite addition to the weekly menu.

1 teaspoon cornstarch
1 large egg
⅔ cup (73 g) finely chopped pecans
⅔ cup (77 g) gluten-free bread crumbs
1 teaspoon salt
½ teaspoon dried oregano
½ teaspoon paprika
¼ teaspoon cayenne pepper
¼ teaspoon black pepper
1 pound (455 g) chicken tenders
½ cup (120 ml) olive oil
Prepared honey-mustard, for serving

Combine the cornstarch and egg in a shallow dish; set aside. Combine the pecans, bread crumbs, salt, oregano, paprika, cayenne pepper, and black pepper in another shallow dish.

Dredge the chicken tenders in the egg mixture and then dredge in the pecan mixture. Place the tenders on a rack to sit while the oil heats.

Heat the oil in a large skillet over medium-high heat until hot. Cook the dredged tenders in hot oil for 3 minutes on each side or until cooked through. Cook in 2 batches, if necessary. Serve with honey-mustard for dipping, if desired.

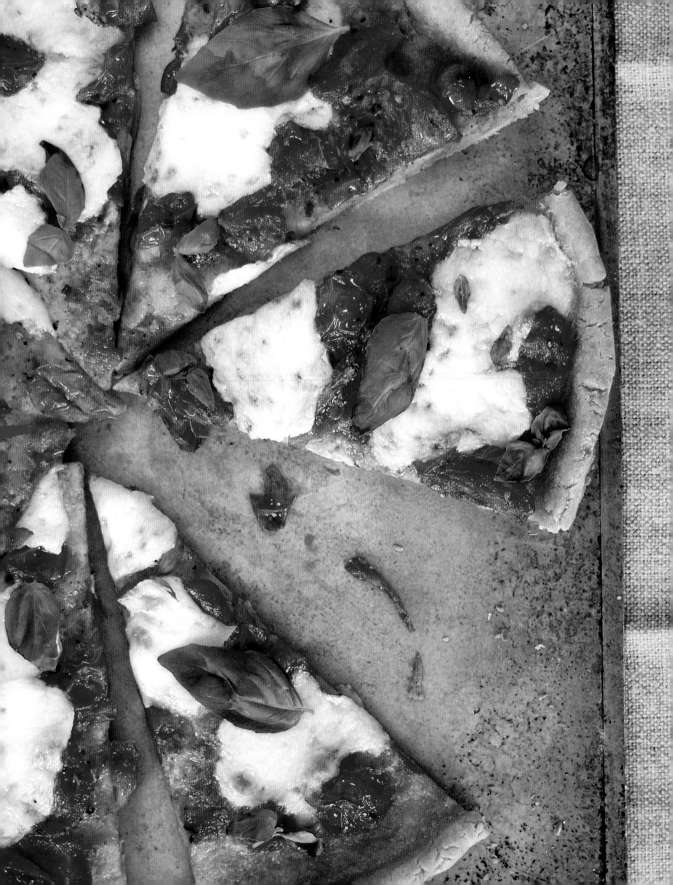

Pizza Margherita

Sometimes you just crave a classic. This simple, traditional pizza combines some of Italy's best flavors. No wonder it's been famous for more than 100 years.

2 tablespoons (30 ml) olive oil

1 pint (551 ml) grape tomatoes

2 cloves garlic, crushed

¼ teaspoon salt

¼ teaspoon black pepper

⅛ teaspoon crushed red pepper flakes

1 recipe Kumquat's Pizza Dough (page 141) or prepared gluten-free pizza dough, rolled out and unbaked

Olive oil for brushing

½ teaspoon garlic powder

8 ounces (227 g) mozzarella cheese balls (*ciliegine*)

½ cup (10 g) basil leaves, for garnish

Preheat oven to 450° (230°C, or gas mark 8).

Heat the olive oil in a large skillet over medium-high heat. Add the tomatoes and garlic; cook until tomatoes burst and release juices. Stir in the salt, pepper, and crushed red pepper.

Place the pizza dough on a baking sheet or pizza stone. Brush evenly with olive oil and sprinkle evenly with the garlic powder. Spread the tomato mixture evenly over the rolled-out pizza crust. Top evenly with the mozzarella cheese balls.

Bake for 16 minutes or until the cheese is melted. Top with the basil leaves. Cut into slices.

Pork Chops & Sauerkraut

I remember my mom making this throughout my childhood to curb the cravings of my German-blooded daddy. Now it's a favorite, comforting one-dish meal in my house too. Be sure to serve with good spicy mustard and gluten-free beer.

2 teaspoons (10 ml) olive oil
4 bone-in pork loin chops
½ teaspoon salt
¼ teaspoon black pepper
2 slices bacon, chopped
½ cup (80 g) sliced onions
1 clove garlic, minced
½ cup (63 g) peeled, chopped apple
½ cup (120 ml) apple juice
2 to 3 cups (284 to 426 g) sauerkraut
1 tablespoon (15 ml) apple cider
   vinegar
½ teaspoon caraway seeds
½ teaspoon mustard seeds

Heat the oil in a large skillet over medium-high heat. Sprinkle the pork chops evenly with salt and pepper. Cook the pork chops in hot oil for 3 minutes on each side or until browned. Remove the chops from the pan, set aside, and keep warm.

Add the bacon to the pan and cook for 1 minute or until beginning to crisp. Add the onion, garlic, and apple; cook for 2 minutes. Add the apple juice, scraping browned bits from the bottom of the pan. Add the sauerkraut, vinegar, caraway seeds, and mustard seeds. Cook for 1 minute and return pork chops to the pan. Cook 2 to 3 minutes or until the pork chops are cooked to desired degree of doneness.

✸ FAST & SIMPLE SUGGESTION ✸

Using kitchen shears, cut raw bacon directly into the pan for quick work and less cleanup.

Pork Tacos with Avocado & Tomato Salsa

YIELD: 8 SERVINGS

Because not all tacos should be beef . . . perfectly spiced and tender pork tenderloin fills these favorites. It's a quick, easy, and tasty weeknight meal.

½ cup (80 g) chopped onion
2 teaspoons (10 ml) olive oil
1 pound (455 g) pork tenderloin, trimmed and coarsely chopped
2 teaspoons (5 g) chili powder
1 teaspoon dried oregano
1 teaspoon garlic powder
½ teaspoon dried thyme
½ teaspoon paprika
¾ teaspoon salt, divided
½ teaspoon black pepper, divided
¼ cup (60 ml) water
½ cup (73 g) chopped avocadoes
½ cup (90 g) chopped tomatoes
¼ cup (40 g) chopped red onion
¼ cup (11 g) chopped cilantro
8 (6-inch, or 15-cm) corn tortillas
Sour cream, for serving

Cook the ½ cup (80 g) onion in hot oil in a large skillet over medium-high heat for 2 minutes. Add the pork to the pan; sprinkle the pork with the chili powder, oregano, garlic powder, thyme, paprika, ½ teaspoon salt, and ¼ teaspoon pepper. Cook for 4 minutes, stirring occasionally, until browned. Stir in the water; scrape browned bits from the bottom of the pan and cook for an additional 2 minutes or until most of the liquid has evaporated.

Meanwhile, combine the avocadoes, tomatoes, ¼ cup (40 g) red onion, cilantro, remaining salt, and remaining pepper in a small bowl.

Warm the tortillas according to package directions. Spoon the pork mixture evenly into each tortilla. Top each evenly with the avocado mixture and sour cream.

✳ DID YOU KNOW? ✳

Many taco seasoning packets contain gluten. This recipe calls for a few easy herbs and spices that result in the delicious, fresh taco flavor we all love and expect, with no hidden gluten.

Red Beans & Rice with Andouille Sausage

YIELD: 4 SERVINGS

This meal has been a comforting favorite of mine since my college days. Spicy sausage, seasoned veggies, and canned beans make for a simple meal that warms you to your toes. I've given a range on the spice, so season the pot with as much heat as you can handle.

1 tablespoon (15 ml) olive oil

12 ounces (340 g) gluten-free andouille sausage, sliced into ¼-inch (6 mm) slices

1 cup (160 g) coarsely chopped red onion

½ cup (75 g) coarsely chopped green pepper

½ cup (50 g) coarsely chopped celery

2 cloves garlic, minced

1 to 2 teaspoons gluten-free Creole seasoning

½ teaspoon dried basil

½ teaspoon salt

½ teaspoon black pepper

1 cup (235 ml) gluten-free chicken broth

1 can (16 ounces, or 453 g) red beans, drained and rinsed

3 tablespoons (8 g) chopped parsley

4 cups (780 g) cooked brown rice

Heat the olive oil in a large skillet over medium-high heat. Add the sausage and cook for 5 minutes, or until sausage begins to brown. Remove the sausage from the skillet with a slotted spoon and keep warm. Add the red onion, green pepper, celery, garlic, Creole seasoning, basil, salt, and pepper; cook for 2 minutes. Add the chicken broth and scrape any browned bits from the bottom of the pan. Add the red beans, cover, and cook for 4 minutes. Partially mash the beans. Add the parsley, and return the sausage and any drippings to the skillet. Simmer for 3 minutes, or until the sauce thickens slightly. Serve over brown rice.

✳ FAST & SIMPLE SUGGESTION ✳

The French term *mise en place* translates to "everything in place," and refers to organizing all ingredients and equipment needed before beginning to cook. It's a particularly helpful technique to use in this recipe, especially for the veggies and seasonings, as it makes cooking a cinch.

Red Lentil Dal

Dal is a traditional Indian stew-like dish made of lentils, typically served over cooked rice. This easy and flavorful dish is a delicious, vegetarian, high-protein answer to "What's for dinner?" It's one of my son's favorites, for sure.

3 cups (705 ml) gluten-free chicken broth
1 cup (192 g) red lentils, rinsed
1 tablespoon (15 ml) olive oil
1½ cups (240 g) very thinly sliced onion
2 cloves garlic, minced
1 teaspoon turmeric
1 teaspoon garam masala
1 teaspoon cumin
½ teaspoon salt
⅛ teaspoon cayenne pepper
1 cup (180 g) diced tomatoes
¼ cup (11 g) chopped cilantro
4 cups (780 g) cooked basmati rice

Bring the broth and lentils to a boil in a medium saucepan. Reduce heat, cover, and simmer for 10 minutes or until the lentils are soft.

Meanwhile, heat the olive oil in a large cast-iron skillet over medium-high to high heat until hot. Add the onions and cook for 8 to 10 minutes or until the onions begin to char, stirring occasionally. Add the garlic and cook for 30 seconds. Add the turmeric, garam masala, cumin, and salt; cook for 30 seconds. Add the lentils, cooking broth, cayenne pepper, and tomatoes to the pan, scraping browned bits from the bottom of the pan. Simmer for 6 minutes, stirring occasionally, or until the juices are reduced and the mixture thickens. Stir in the cilantro.

Serve over basmati rice.

✹ DID YOU KNOW? ✹

Garam masala is a delicious, aromatic blend of spices that is essential to the flavors of classic Indian cooking. This exotic blend typically combines coriander, cumin, cardamom, cinnamon, black pepper, and other spices.

Roasted Salmon & Asparagus with Lemon-Caper-Dill Aioli

YIELD: 4 (ABOUT 6-OUNCE, OR 170 G) SERVINGS

Here's a brilliant and simple method for cooking your whole meal at once, with only one pan to clean. Roasting gives both the asparagus and the salmon a wonderful complex flavor. And the fresh, lemony, short-cut aioli is the perfect partner to this roasted pair.

FOR SALMON AND ASPARAGUS:

1 pound (455 g) asparagus, trimmed
Cooking spray
1 tablespoon (15 ml) olive oil
½ teaspoon salt, divided
¼ teaspoon black pepper, divided
1½ pounds (680 g) skinless
 salmon fillet

FOR AIOLI:

¾ cup (175 g) mayonnaise
1 clove garlic, minced
1 teaspoon finely grated organic
 lemon rind
1 tablespoon (15 ml) lemon juice
1 tablespoon (4 g) finely chopped
 fresh dill
1 tablespoon (9 g) chopped capers
2 teaspoons (7 g) finely minced
 red onion
¼ teaspoon salt
¼ teaspoon black pepper

To make the make the salmon and asparagus: Preheat oven to 450°F (230°C, or gas mark 8).

Arrange the asparagus in an even layer on a rimmed baking sheet coated with cooking spray. Drizzle with the olive oil and sprinkle with half the salt and pepper. Place the salmon fillet directly on top of the asparagus. Sprinkle with the remaining salt and pepper.

Roast the salmon for 18 minutes or until the fish flakes when tested with a fork.

To make the aioli: Meanwhile, combine the mayonnaise and the remaining ingredients in a small bowl until well blended. Serve the salmon and asparagus with aioli.

Shrimp Spring Rolls

YIELD: 5 SERVINGS

Fresh spring rolls are a refreshing and elegant change from the fried version. They are easy and fun to make, and packed with crunchy, delicious vegetables. These would make a fantastic, light, and delicious summer meal.

1 ounce (29 g) thin rice noodles

10 rounds rice paper wrappers

10 teaspoons (50 ml) gluten-free hoisin sauce, divided

1¼ cups (55 g) sliced green leaf lettuce, divided

⅔ cup (33 g) bean sprouts, divided

⅔ cup (73 g) shredded carrots, divided

20 basil leaves, divided

¼ cup (4 g) cilantro leaves, divided

10 cooked medium shrimp, halved lengthwise, divided

Gluten-free sweet red chili sauce, such as Thai Kitchen, for serving

Pour boiling water over the rice noodles; stir to separate and let sit until tender, 2 minutes. Drain, rinse with cold water until cool, and drain again. Using scissors, cut the noodles into 3-inch (7.5 cm) lengths.

Pour 1 inch (2.5 cm) hot tap water into a large, shallow bowl. Submerge 1 rice paper wrapper in the water until flexible and tender, about 30 seconds. Place the wrapper on a clean counter or cutting board and top it with 1 teaspoon (5 ml) hoisin sauce, 2 tablespoons (22 g) rice noodles, 2 tablespoons (5 g) lettuce, 1 tablespoon (7 g) bean sprouts, 1 tablespoon carrots (7 g), 2 basil leaves, and 1 teaspoon cilantro. Fold in the sides. Begin to roll up lengthwise, placing 2 halves of shrimp in the wrapper as it is rolled up.

Repeat with the remaining wrappers and fillings. Serve immediately with sweet red chili sauce.

✳ RECIPE TIP: USE ORGANIC CITRUS ✳

When zesting, grating, or using the whole fruit, always use organic citrus. Pesticides and sprays remain on the skins of the fruits, so when the peel will be removed and discarded and only the segments of the fruit eaten, it's not quite as important to choose organic. When using both the zest and juice of a citrus fruit, always zest first.

Spaghetti & Meatballs

I've given the iconic favorite a gluten-free makeover, and the result is a scrumptious, flavorful crowd pleaser . . . because we all need a delicious recipe for spaghetti and meatballs in our dinner arsenal.

1 package (12 ounces, or 340 g) gluten-free spaghetti

1 jar (25 ounces, or 709 g) gluten-free tomato-basil pasta sauce, divided

¼ cup (25 g) grated Parmesan cheese

2 teaspoons (2 g) chopped fresh basil

½ teaspoon garlic powder

½ teaspoon salt

¼ teaspoon black pepper

1 pound (455 g) ground beef

Parmesan cheese, for garnish

Chopped fresh basil, for garnish

Cook the pasta according to package instructions.

Place ⅓ cup (87 g) pasta sauce in a medium bowl. Bring the remainder of the pasta sauce to a boil in a large saucepan; reduce heat and simmer gently.

Meanwhile, add the Parmesan cheese, basil, garlic powder, salt, and pepper to the pasta sauce in the bowl and mix. Add the ground beef and mix with hands. Roll into tight 2-inch (5 cm) balls.

Add the meatballs to the simmering sauce, cover the saucepan, and cook for 5 to 7 minutes, or until the meatballs are cooked through, occasionally stirring gently.

Serve the meatballs and sauce over cooked pasta. Top with additional Parmesan cheese and chopped fresh basil, if desired.

Tempura Shrimp with Sweet Chili Sauce

YIELD: 4 SERVINGS

These Japanese-style fried shrimp, with their light and crunchy coating, are sure to impress both in look and taste. You'll never, ever miss the gluten.

FOR TEMPURA SHRIMP:
Canola oil
½ cup (60 grams) tapioca flour
½ cup (65 grams) cornstarch
¼ cup (35 grams) rice flour
1 teaspoon baking powder
½ teaspoon garlic powder
¼ teaspoon salt
⅛ teaspoon cayenne pepper
½ cup (120 ml) ice cold water
1 pound (455 g) jumbo shrimp
   (16–20 count), shells peeled,
   tails on

FOR SWEET CHILI SAUCE:
⅓ cup (92 g) gluten-free sweet red chili
   sauce, such as Thai Kitchen
2 tablespoons (30 ml) rice vinegar
2 teaspoons (10 ml) fresh lime juice

To make the tempura shrimp: Add the canola oil to a heavy-duty saucepan to measure 3 inches (7.5 cm) up the sides of the pan. Heat to 370°F (188°C), measuring with a candy thermometer.

While the oil heats, combine the tapioca flour, cornstarch, rice flour, baking powder, garlic powder, salt, and cayenne pepper in a medium bowl. Add the cold water and stir with a wire whisk until smooth. (Add additional cold water, if necessary, to make a thick batter.)

Hold the tail of a shrimp and dip into the batter; immediately place dipped shrimp into the hot oil. Fry 2 minutes on each side or until slightly browned. Remove with a slotted spoon and drain on paper towels. Repeat with remaining shrimp and batter, stirring batter occasionally and frying in batches.

To make the sweet chili sauce: Combine the sweet red chili sauce, rice vinegar, and lime juice in a small bowl. Stir to combine well.

Serve the shrimp immediately with Sweet Chili Sauce.

CHAPTER 5

Speedy Soups & Salads

MANY SUMMER NIGHTS OUR DINNER CONSISTS OF IMPROMPTU SALADS, always using fresh, cold greens, nuts, dried or fresh fruits, cheese, and meats. Really, it's often whatever I have in the fridge and pantry that will complement each other. In these recipes I've taken the guesswork out of the salad bowl and provided a few of my favorites that are perfect for the warmer spring and summer months—or really any time of year. Throw in a warm, flavorful bowl of soup, and I'm very satisfied. This chapter is full of both of these. Make a meal out of any pairing you please and relish the time free from slaving over a sink of dirty dishes!

Chocolate Chili

Similar to a Mexican mole, the chocolate in this chili provides richness and depth of flavor more than it provides sweetness. Mix up a pot on a cool, fall day and serve with the Honey Skillet Cornbread on page 118. Your heart and your belly will be happy.

1 pound (455 g) ground beef

1 cup (160 g) chopped onion

2 cloves garlic, minced

1 can (14.5 ounces, or 411 g) crushed fire-roasted tomatoes, undrained

1 can (14 ounces, or 397 g) pinto beans, drained and rinsed

½ jalapeño pepper, seeded and minced

1 can (14 ounces, or 425 ml) gluten-free chicken broth

2 tablespoons (15 g) chili powder

2 ounces (57 g) semisweet chocolate, chopped

1½ teaspoons (4 g) cumin

1½ teaspoons (9 g) salt

1 teaspoon dried oregano

½ teaspoon black pepper

Sour cream, for serving

Shredded Cheddar cheese, for serving

Scallions, for serving

Cook the beef, onion, and garlic in a large saucepan over medium-high heat for 7 minutes or until beef is browned, stirring occasionally to crumble. Drain, if necessary. Add the tomatoes, pinto beans, jalapeño, chicken broth, chili powder, chocolate, cumin, salt, oregano, and pepper to the pan. Bring to a boil and cook for 5 to 7 minutes or until thickened. Serve immediately, topped with sour cream, Cheddar cheese, and scallions, if desired.

Red Curry Chicken Soup

Oooooo, this one's good. Rich coconut milk and spicy red curry is a perfect combination for this Thai soup. All of the flavorful and aromatic ingredients blend together beautifully to result in a truly satisfying one-dish meal. The curry packs a punch, so I've given a range for you to determine what your tongue can handle.

2 tablespoons (30 ml) olive oil

¼ cup (40 g) sliced shallots

1 tablespoon (6 g) peeled and minced fresh ginger

2 cloves garlic, minced

1 to 2 tablespoons (15 to 30 g) red curry paste

1 teaspoon curry powder

½ teaspoon ground coriander

4 cups (940 ml) gluten-free chicken broth

1 can (13.5 ounces, or 398 ml) unsweetened coconut milk

2 cups (280 g) chopped, cooked chicken

1 cup (70 g) sliced mushrooms

1 cup (98 g) snow peas

½ cup (50 g) chopped scallions

2 tablespoons (26 g) sugar

2 tablespoons (30 ml) fish sauce (*nam pla*)

2 tablespoons (30 ml) lime juice

3 tablespoons (8 g) chopped cilantro, for serving

3 tablespoons (8 g) chopped basil, for serving

Heat the oil in a large saucepan or Dutch oven over medium-high heat. Add the shallots and cook for 1 minute. Add the ginger and garlic and cook for 1 minute. Add the red curry paste, curry powder, and coriander. Stir in the chicken broth and coconut milk. Bring to a boil, reduce heat, and bring to a simmer. Add the chicken, mushrooms, snow peas, scallions, sugar, and fish sauce. Cook until heated through. Remove from heat; stir in the lime juice. Serve, topped evenly with cilantro and basil.

Tortilla Chicken Soup

This soup makes the comfort food list for this Texas girl. It also makes the quick and easy list too. So, it's a win-win! It's a simple dump-and-stir soup, but the homemade tortilla strips steal the show.

4 (6-inch, or 15 cm) corn tortillas
Cooking spray
1¾ teaspoons (4.3 g) cumin, divided
1¾ teaspoons (10.5 g) salt, divided
1 tablespoon (15 ml) olive oil
½ cup (80 g) chopped onion
1 clove garlic, minced
½ jalapeño pepper, seeded and minced
4 cups (940 ml) gluten-free chicken broth
1 can (14.5 ounces, or 411 g) crushed fire-roasted tomatoes, undrained
1 can (15 ounces, or 425 g) black beans, rinsed and drained
½ teaspoon chili powder
2 cups (280 g) chopped, cooked chicken
Avocado, for serving
Chopped cilantro, for serving
Shredded Monterey Jack cheese, for serving
Lime wedges, for serving

Preheat oven to 425°F (220°C, or gas mark 7). Cut the tortillas into ¼-inch (6 mm)-thick strips. Place the strips on a baking sheet coated with cooking spray. Spray the strips with the cooking spray and then sprinkle evenly with ¼ teaspoon cumin and ¼ teaspoon salt. Bake for 10 minutes or until golden and crisp, stirring once.

Meanwhile, heat the olive oil in a large saucepan over medium-high heat. Cook the onion, garlic, and jalapeño for 2 minutes. Add the broth, tomatoes, black beans, remaining cumin, remaining salt, and chili powder to the pan. Bring to a simmer. Add the chicken and cook for 3 minutes or until heated through. Ladle into bowls, and top with tortilla strips, avocado, cilantro, and Monterey Jack cheese. Serve with lime wedges.

✴ RECIPE TIP: SPRAY SAFE ✴

Be certain to avoid the cooking sprays that are intended for "baking." These contain wheat flour and are not gluten-free. Make sure the aerosol cooking spray you buy is gluten-free.

Fish Chowder

This is traditional New England chowder at its best . . . thick and creamy, full of fish and potatoes, flavored with a perfect blend of vegetables and bacon. It's a hearty, satisfying, simple, and delicious.

6 slices bacon

2 cups (320 g) chopped onion

½ cup (50 g) chopped celery

½ cup (65 g) chopped carrots

2 tablespoons (16 g) Kumquat's Gluten-Free All-Purpose Flour Blend (page 15) or gluten-free all-purpose flour

3 cups (705 ml) gluten-free chicken broth

2 bay leaves

1 pound (455 g) baking potatoes, peeled and cut into ½-inch (12 mm) pieces

1 cup (235 ml) half and half

1 teaspoon dried thyme

1 teaspoon salt

½ teaspoon black pepper

1 pound (455 g) tilapia fillets, cut into 1-inch (2.5 cm) chunks

Cook the bacon in a Dutch oven or large saucepan over medium-high heat until crisp. Remove with a slotted spoon and set aside. Add the onion, celery, and carrots to the bacon fat in the pan and cook for 3 minutes. Stir in the flour and cook for 1 minute. Stir in the chicken broth, scraping browned bits from the bottom of the pan. Add the bay leaves and potatoes. Bring to a boil and cook, covered, for 5 minutes or until potatoes are just tender. Add the half and half, thyme, salt, pepper, and fish. Cook for 5 minutes or until the fish is cooked through.

Before serving, remove and discard the bay leaves. Crumble the reserved bacon and serve on top of each serving.

✳ DID YOU KNOW? ✳

Despite what you would imagine, not all store-bought chicken broth is gluten-free. Many brands manufacture their broths in plants that also manufacture products made with wheat. Be certain to confirm that the broth you buy contains no wheat and is manufactured in a gluten-free facility.

Rustic Italian Salad with Grilled Chicken

YIELD: 4 TO 6 SERVINGS

This is the ultimate salad. Mixed in are all of my very favorite Italian flavors. Roasted grapes, toasted pine nuts, chewy sun-dried tomatoes, salty prosciutto and Parmesan . . . they're all divine and mouthwatering. All that's needed is a cool glass of white wine and some warm sunlight.

¼ cup (60 ml) plus 2 tablespoons (30 ml) olive oil, divided
2½ ounces (70 g) prosciutto, coarsely chopped
1½ cup (225 g) red grapes
½ apple, cored and thinly sliced
½ cup (55 g) chopped sun-dried tomatoes in oil, drained
⅓ cup (45 g) pine nuts, toasted
⅓ cup (33 g) shaved Parmesan cheese
¼ cup (40 g) minced red onion
8 cups (440 g) mixed greens
2 cups (300 g) sliced, grilled chicken breast
1 tablespoon (15 ml) lemon juice
1 tablespoon (15 ml) balsamic vinegar
1 teaspoon Dijon mustard
¼ teaspoon salt
¼ teaspoon black pepper

Heat 2 tablespoons (30 ml) olive oil in a large skillet. Add the prosciutto and cook for 3 minutes or until crisp. Remove with a slotted spoon and keep warm. Add the grapes to the pan and cook for 3 minutes or until the grapes' skins begin to burst.

Combine the prosciutto, grapes, apple, sun-dried tomatoes, pine nuts, Parmesan cheese, and red onion in a large salad bowl. Toss with the mixed greens and chicken.

Combine the remaining olive oil, lemon juice, balsamic vinegar, Dijon mustard, salt, and pepper in a bowl or measuring cup. Pour dressing over salad and toss to coat. Serve immediately.

✷ RECIPE TIP: TOAST PINE NUTS TO PERFECTION ✷

To toast pine nuts, bake them at 350°F (180°C, or gas mark 4) for 6 to 8 minutes. Or cook them in a skillet for 1 to 2 minutes, or until fragrant and just browned.

Arugula Salad with Oranges, Pomegranate Seeds & Parmesan Rounds

YIELD: 4 SERVINGS

I love the mixture of peppery arugula, sweet pomegranate seeds, juicy citrus, and salty cheese in this flavorful salad. The colors mix together beautifully in your salad bowl, and the presentation is fancy enough for a dinner party.

FOR PARMESAN ROUNDS:
¾ cup (75 g) grated Parmesan cheese

FOR DRESSING:
⅓ cup (75 ml) olive oil
3 tablespoons (45 ml) champagne
   vinegar
1 teaspoon Dijon mustard
1 teaspoon fresh pomegranate juice
1 teaspoon fresh orange juice
¼ teaspoon salt
⅛ teaspoon black pepper

FOR SALAD:
6 cups (120 g) baby arugula
2 oranges, segmented
1 cup (100 g) walnut halves, toasted
½ cup (80 g) pomegranate seeds

To make the Parmesan rounds: Preheat oven to 350°F (180°C, or gas mark 4).

Place a 2-inch (5 cm) cookie cutter on a parchment-lined baking sheet. Sprinkle 1 tablespoon (5 g) Parmesan cheese evenly inside of cookie cutter. Lift cutter to create even round of Parmesan cheese. Repeat with remaining Parmesan cheese. Bake for 6 minutes. Remove parchment from hot baking sheet for faster cooling.

To make the dressing: Combine the olive oil, champagne vinegar, mustard, pomegranate juice, orange juice, salt, and pepper in small bowl or measuring cup. Stir mixture vigorously to combine.

To make the salad: Combine the arugula, orange segments, walnuts, and pomegranate seeds in a medium bowl. Toss with dressing. Divide evenly among 4 plates. Top each portion with Parmesan Rounds.

✳ RECIPE TIP: HOW TO "SUPREME" AN ORANGE ✳

Orange segments without any skin, pith, membrane or seeds are also called "supremes." To achieve this technique, first cut off a little of the top and bottom of the orange with a sharp knife. Then trim away the skin, being sure to remove the white pith but leaving as much of the fruit intact as possible. Working over a bowl, slip the knife on either side of each membrane and release each segment of fruit, catching orange segments in the bowl; discard membrane.

Quinoa Tabbouleh

Substituting high-protein quinoa for traditional bulgur makes this refreshing Lebanese salad gluten-free. Crunchy pine nuts, chewy quinoa and currants, fresh herbs, and tangy lemon make an ideal combination. It is delicious when served immediately, but even better when chilled overnight, allowing the flavors to blend.

1 cup (173 g) quinoa
¾ teaspoon salt
½ teaspoon black pepper
2 cloves garlic, minced
¼ cup (60 ml) olive oil
3 tablespoons (45 ml) lemon juice
1 cup (45 g) chopped fresh curly parsley
¼ cup (12 g) chopped fresh mint
½ cup (70 g) seeded, chopped
   cucumber
½ cup (90 g) seeded, chopped tomato
¼ cup (25 g) chopped scallions
¼ cup (38 g) currants
¼ cup (35 g) toasted pine nuts

Cook the quinoa according to package instructions. Cool slightly. Stir in the remaining ingredients. Serve immediately or, if desired, chill before serving.

✳ RECIPE TIP: KEEP HERBS FRESH ✳

To store fresh herbs like parsley and mint, freshly cut the stems when you get them home from the grocery store, wrap the stems with a wet paper towel, and place in the refrigerator in a large zip-top plastic bag.

Tarragon-Lemon Chicken Salad

YIELD: 4 (8-OUNCE, OR 225 G) SERVINGS

I have fond memories of fun, laid-back lunches at a little French bistro years ago. They always served the most delicious tarragon-lemon chicken salad. Since then, I've done my best to re-create their dish. It's tart, tangy, and herby and perfect for your own laid-back lunch.

3½ cups (490 g) chopped chicken, pulled from rotisserie chicken
¼ cup (40 g) diced red onion
½ cup (115 g) mayonnaise
2 tablespoons (30 ml) fresh lemon juice
1 tablespoon (11 g) Dijon mustard
1 tablespoon (4 g) chopped fresh tarragon
1 teaspoon organic lemon zest
1 teaspoon heavy cream
½ teaspoon salt
¼ teaspoon garlic powder
¼ teaspoon black pepper

Combine all the ingredients in a large bowl, and stir well. Serve immediately or chill.

✳ RECIPE TIP ✳

When using dried herbs in place of fresh, use a 3 to 1 ratio, which means if a recipe calls for 3 teaspoons (4 g) fresh herbs, use 1 teaspoon dried herbs. However, in recipes that require no cook time, such as this salad, fresh herbs are best. Dried herbs are best for recipes that require long cook times, such as soups and stews.

6

Super-Quick Sides

➤ **SIDE DISHES ARE OFTEN WHERE THE BULK OF THE VEGETABLES ARE FOUND ON OUR PLATES.** Because so many people who cannot eat gluten often struggle with gastrointestinal issues, it is important to consume high-fiber, nutrient-rich foods such as vegetables and whole grains. These foods supplement the body with needed vitamins and minerals, as well as keep things healthy and moving in the intestines. Luckily, I enjoy most vegetables, but I still want them to be as flavorful as they are nutritious. The ones I've included here deserve a bright spotlight. I've included old favorites, like Four-Cheese Baked Macaroni & Cheese (page 102) as well as Indian-Spiced Peas (page 104). I hope you love them all!

Four-Cheese Baked Macaroni & Cheese

This family favorite is back on your gluten-free plate and has never been easier. This ultimate, extra-cheesy, classic comfort dish will definitely warm your belly and your soul.

3 cups (315 g) uncooked gluten-free elbow pasta
½ cup (58 g) shredded Cheddar cheese
½ cup (55 g) shredded Muenster cheese
½ cup (58 g) shredded Colby cheese
½ cup (55 g) shredded Swiss cheese
2 large eggs
1 cup (235 ml) evaporated milk
⅓ cup (77 g) sour cream
3 tablespoons (45 g) butter, melted
½ teaspoon dried mustard
½ teaspoon salt
¼ teaspoon black pepper
Cooking spray

Preheat oven to 400°F (200°C, or gas mark 6).

Cook the pasta according to package directions until al dente in boiling salted water, about 10 minutes. Drain the pasta and transfer to a large bowl. Add the four cheeses to the hot pasta and stir to melt.

Meanwhile, combine the eggs, milk, sour cream, melted butter, mustard, salt, and pepper in a medium bowl. Stir the milk mixture into the cheesy pasta.

Pour the pasta mixture into a 9-inch (23 cm) square baking dish coated with cooking spray. Bake for 15 to 20 minutes or until lightly golden. Sprinkle with additional cheese, if desired. Serve immediately.

✳ DID YOU KNOW? ✳

Is there a difference between a baking dish and a pan? Why, yes, there is! "Baking dish" refers to a glass dish, whereas "pan" refers to a metal pan. Glass and metal conduct heat differently, so use what is called for in recipes to avoid over- or undercooking the food.

Broccoli Salad

Here is the ultimate way to eat your broccoli. With a touch of sweetness, a crunch of salty, and a bit of tangy, it is simple and truly addicting.

½ cup (115 g) mayonnaise
2 tablespoons (26 g) sugar
1 tablespoon (15 ml) apple cider
　vinegar
8 slices bacon, cooked and crumbled
½ cup diced (66 g) Cheddar cheese
⅓ cup (53 g) diced red onion
¼ teaspoon salt
¼ teaspoon black pepper
4 cups (284 g) raw broccoli florets

Combine all the ingredients, except the broccoli florets, in a medium bowl. Stir in the broccoli. Serve room temperature or chilled.

✳ FAST & SIMPLE SUGGESTION ✳

Buying already prepared florets will save you lots of chopping time.

Greens Sauté

This delicious side dish is this Southern girl's favorite way to eat her greens. Loaded with vitamins, fiber, and flavor, this sauté is healthy and delightful.

3 slices bacon, coarsely chopped
⅓ cup (35 g) thinly sliced shallots
1 clove garlic, minced
¼ teaspoon red pepper flakes
3 tablespoons (45 ml) apple cider
　vinegar
10 ounces (284 g) coarsely chopped
　kale or Swiss chard
2 tablespoons (28 g) butter
¼ teaspoon salt
¼ teaspoon black pepper

Cook the bacon in a large skillet until almost crispy. Add the shallots, garlic, and red pepper flakes. Cook for 2 minutes or until beginning to brown. Add the vinegar and scrape browned bits from the bottom of the pan. Add the kale or Swiss chard and cook for 3 minutes or until wilted. Melt the butter into the mixture. Season with the salt and pepper.

Indian-Spiced Peas

These simple peas are the ultimate in a flavor-packed spoonful. They pair beautifully with grilled meats and cooked rice. Pair with the Red Lentil Dal on page 81 for a mouth-watering Indian feast.

2 tablespoons (30 ml) olive oil
½ cup (65 g) diced, peeled carrots
½ cup (80 g) diced onion
1 clove garlic, minced
½ cup (90 g) chopped tomato
1 package (16 ounces, or 454 g)
    frozen peas, unthawed
1 teaspoon garam masala
½ teaspoon cumin
½ teaspoon salt
¼ teaspoon black pepper

Heat the olive oil in a large skillet until hot. Cook the carrots, onion, and garlic in the hot oil for 4 minutes, or until lightly browned, stirring occasionally. Add the tomato and cook for 1 minute.

Add the peas and cook for 6 minutes, stirring occasionally. Stir in the garam masala, cumin, salt, and pepper. Cook for 1 minute, or until fragrant, stirring occasionally. Serve immediately.

✳ DID YOU KNOW? ✳

Garam masala is a delicious, aromatic blend of spices that is essential to the flavors of classic Indian cooking. This exotic blend typically combines coriander, cumin, cardamom, cinnamon, black pepper, and other spices.

Individual Stuffings with Sausage, Cranberry, Apples & Pecans

YIELD: 8 SERVINGS

All of the very best flavors of fall combine to make this holiday favorite. Individual servings allow them to cook faster and make them an easy make-ahead dish. This tasty recipe graces our Thanksgiving table every year.

½ pound (228 g) fresh nitrate-free pork breakfast sausage
6 tablespoons (84 g) butter
½ cup (80 g) chopped onion
2 ribs celery, chopped
1 cup (125 g) chopped, peeled Granny Smith apple
2 cloves garlic, minced
1 cup (110 g) chopped pecans
1 cup (120 g) dried cranberries
2 teaspoons fresh, minced sage
2 cups (220 g) dried gluten-free bread crumbs, such as Aleia's plain bread crumbs
1 teaspoon salt
½ teaspoon black pepper
1 cup (235 ml) gluten-free chicken broth
Cooking spray

Preheat oven to 400°F (200°C, or gas mark 6).

Cook the sausage in a large skillet over medium-high heat, breaking up the sausage, until browned. Transfer the sausage with a slotted spoon to a large bowl and keep warm. Melt the butter in the sausage drippings in the pan. Add the onion, celery, apple, and garlic; cook for 2 minutes. Remove to the bowl with the sausage.

Add the pecans, cranberries, sage, bread crumbs, salt, and pepper to the bowl; stir well to combine. Stir in the chicken broth to moisten the bread crumbs.

Spoon the mixture evenly among 8 ramekins coated with cooking spray. Place the ramekins on a large rimmed baking sheet. Cover the ramekins with a sheet of aluminum foil. Bake for 10 minutes. Remove the foil and bake for an additional 10 minutes, or until golden brown.

☀ RECIPE TIP: SAY NO TO NITRATES ☀

Nitrates are added to cured meats to prevent bacterial growth and keep the meat looking "fresh." When nitrates are cooked at high temperatures, they are converted to nitrites. These nitrites are believed to cause certain cancers, including stomach, colon, and pancreatic cancer. When purchasing cured meats, look for a product that states "nitrate free" or "no nitrates added."

Fried Green Beans with Horseradish Dipping Sauce

YIELD: 4 SERVINGS

I promise that this will become your favorite way to eat your green beans. The light and crunchy batter, the spicy and delicious sauce . . . you'll have a hard time sharing. Serve as a side dish or an appetizer.

FOR DIPPING SAUCE:

½ cup (115 g) mayonnaise
1 tablespoon (15 g) prepared horseradish, drained
1 tablespoon (15 g) ketchup
½ teaspoon paprika
½ teaspoon garlic powder
½ teaspoon salt
⅛ teaspoon cayenne pepper

FOR GREEN BEANS:

¾ cup (175 ml) buttermilk
1 cup (140 grams) Kumquat's Gluten-Free All-Purpose Flour Blend (page 15) or gluten-free all-purpose flour
1 teaspoon garlic powder
2 teaspoons (12 g) salt
½ teaspoon black pepper
4 cups (940 ml) canola oil
½ pound (228 g) haricot verts or green beans, trimmed

To make the dipping sauce: Combine the mayonnaise, horseradish, ketchup, paprika, garlic powder, salt, and cayenne pepper in a medium bowl. Cover and chill until ready to serve.

To make the green beans: Combine the buttermilk, flour, garlic powder, salt, and pepper in a medium bowl; whisk until smooth. Heat the oil in a large saucepan or Dutch oven to 375°F (190°C) when measured with a candy thermometer. Dip the green beans, in batches, in the batter and fry in the hot oil for 3 minutes or until golden brown. Spoon out of the hot oil with a slotted spoon and drain on paper towels. Serve immediately with dipping sauce.

> ✳ RECIPE TIP: USE A THERMOMETER FOR FRYING SUCCESS ✳
>
> A candy thermometer is a long, metal, high-temperature thermometer that hangs on the side of the saucepan. Use this thermometer for foolproof frying to make sure your oil is the right temperature. Too cool, and you may end up with soggy food. Too hot and you will burn your food and may end up with a kitchen fire.

Garlic, Herb & Bacon Mashed Potatoes

YIELD: 6 TO 8 SERVINGS

Add some garlic, herbed cheese, and bacon and this creamy and comforting classic side is transformed into a spoonful of heaven.

2 pounds (910 g) new potatoes, washed, unpeeled, and cut into ½-inch pieces
10 cloves garlic, skins removed
1 container (5.2 ounces, or 150 g) garlic and herbs spreadable cheese, such as Boursin, softened
2 tablespoons (28 g) butter
½ cup (120 ml) milk or milk alternative
1 teaspoon salt
1 teaspoon black pepper
6 slices bacon, cooked and crumbled

Place the potatoes and garlic in a large saucepan or Dutch oven and fill with water to just cover potatoes. Boil over high heat for 10 to 12 minutes. Drain water. Mash with a fork or potato masher or until potatoes are tender when pierced with a fork.

Stir in the herb cheese, butter, milk, salt, and pepper until well combined. Stir in bacon pieces. Serve immediately.

Ginger-Glazed Carrots

YIELD: 4 SERVINGS

Two constants in my life: the question of what side dish to serve with dinner, and a bag of carrots in my crisper. Luckily, with this recipe, one constant answers the other!

1 pound (455 g) carrots
⅓ cup (75 ml) orange juice
2 tablespoons (28 g) butter
1 tablespoon (15 g) packed brown sugar
2 teaspoons (4 g) peeled and minced fresh ginger
¼ teaspoon salt
⅛ teaspoon black pepper

Peel carrots and cut on the diagonal into ¼-inch (6 mm) slices. Combine the carrots, orange juice, butter, brown sugar, and ginger in a large skillet. Simmer over medium-high heat for 5 minutes or until liquid evaporates and the carrots are cooked and glazed. Sprinkle evenly with the salt and pepper.

Roasted Beets with Red Onion, Walnuts & Dill

YIELD: 4 SERVINGS

Oh, how I love beets and their earthy flavor, but not everyone does. To please the crowds, roasting beets pulls out their natural sweetness and softens their texture. Paired with roasted red onions, crunchy walnuts, and a hint of dill, they are the perfect side for a fall meal.

¾ pound (341 g) beets, each peeled and cut into eighths
1 medium red onion, cut into 1-inch (2.5 cm) pieces
¼ cup (60 ml) olive oil, divided
½ cup (60 g) toasted, chopped walnuts
2 teaspoons (3 g) chopped fresh dill
1 teaspoon champagne vinegar
½ teaspoon salt
¼ teaspoon black pepper

Preheat oven to 450°F (230°C, or gas mark 8).

Place the beets and red onion on a large rimmed baking sheet. Drizzle evenly with 2 tablespoons (30 ml) olive oil. Roast for 20 minutes or until the edges begin to brown, stirring once halfway through cooking.

Toss the beets and onion in a large bowl with the walnuts, dill, vinegar, salt, and pepper. Serve immediately.

> ✳ RECIPE TIP: TOAST WALNUTS
> TO PERFECTION ✳
>
> To toast walnuts, bake them at 350°F (180°C, or gas mark 4) for 6 to 8 minutes. Or cook them in a skillet for 1 to 2 minutes or until fragrant and just browned.

Roasted Asparagus in Browned Butter

YIELD: 4 SERVINGS

Roasting asparagus is one of my favorite ways to bring out the best flavors of the vegetable. Finished with browned butter and a hint of lemon, these will become your favorite and easiest go-to side dish.

1 pound (455 g) asparagus, trimmed
1 tablespoon (15 ml) olive oil
2 tablespoons (28 g) butter
½ teaspoon salt
¼ teaspoon black pepper
1 teaspoon fresh organic lemon zest

Preheat oven to 450°F (230°C, or gas mark 8).

Toss the asparagus with olive oil on a rimmed baking sheet. Roast the asparagus for 10 minutes, stirring once, halfway through roasting.

Meanwhile, heat the butter in a small skillet over medium heat until just browned, stirring occasionally. Remove from heat.

Toss the asparagus with the browned butter, salt, pepper, and lemon zest. Serve immediately.

Spanish Rice

YIELD: 4 TO 6 (5-OUNCE, OR 125 G) SERVINGS

No Tex-Mex plate is complete without a heaping helping of Spanish Rice. This is the one I make at my house. It pairs perfectly with the Green Chicken Enchiladas on page 62.

3 tablespoons (45 ml) bacon fat or olive oil
1 cup (195 g) uncooked white rice
½ cup (80 g) chopped onion
1 clove garlic, minced
1 can (14.5 ounces, or 411 g) diced tomatoes
1 teaspoon cumin
1 teaspoon salt
½ teaspoon oregano
½ teaspoon black pepper
1 can (14 ounces, or 425 ml) gluten-free chicken broth

Heat the bacon fat or olive oil in a large skillet with a lid, uncovered, over medium-high heat. Add the rice to the hot fat and cook for 2 minutes, stirring occasionally. Add the onion and garlic and cook for 1 minute. Stir in the remaining ingredients. Bring to a boil, reduce heat, cover, and simmer for 14 minutes or until liquid is absorbed and the rice is tender. Serve immediately.

Sautéed Brussels Sprouts with Cranberries & Walnuts

YIELD: 4 SERVINGS

If you aren't a fan of the Brussels sprout, it's probably because you've not had them cooked properly. Be sure to allow them to brown a bit in the pan. This lets the sprouts caramelize and turns any bitterness to deliciousness. Oh, they're so delightful. You have to try them.

3 slices bacon, coarsely chopped

1 pound (455 g) Brussels sprouts, rinsed, trimmed, and quartered

⅓ cup (40 g) coarsely chopped walnuts

⅓ cup (40 g) dried cranberries

⅓ cup (33 g) chopped scallions

2 tablespoons (30 ml) gluten-free chicken broth

1 tablespoon (15 ml) apple cider vinegar

½ teaspoon salt

¼ teaspoon black pepper

2 tablespoons (28 g) butter

¼ cup (20 g) shredded Parmesan cheese, for garnish

Cook the bacon in a large skillet over medium-high heat for 3 minutes or until almost crispy. Add the Brussels sprouts and cook, covered, stirring occasionally, for 5 minutes or until they begin to brown. Add the walnuts, cranberries, and scallions; cook for 2 minutes. Add the chicken broth and vinegar, scraping browned bits from the bottom of the pan. Add the salt and pepper and then melt the butter into the mixture. Sprinkle with the Parmesan cheese. Serve immediately.

✳ FAST & SIMPLE SUGGESTION ✳

To trim Brussels sprouts, simply cut off the bottom ⅛-inch of the stem and remove and discard any loose or wilted outer leaves, which should fall away easily.

CHAPTER 7

Daily Bread (in Minutes)

➤ **BREADS ARE THE ONE FOOD YOU MAY HAVE THOUGHT YOU WOULD NEVER EAT AGAIN.** But here they are . . . flakey, buttery, tender, fragrant, easy. So get yourself a new bread basket because it's about to be filled. Savory biscuits, cornbread, and homemade tortillas are perfect with fall soups and chilis. Sweet Orange Biscuits (page 121) are a beautiful and welcome addition to a brunch menu or just enjoy one with a cup of hot tea or coffee. You'll also find some basic recipes for easy pie crusts to be used in a few other recipes throughout the book. Or use them to make your own favorite family pies and quiches gluten-free, but just as delicious as you remembered them. Are you drooling yet?

Handmade Corn Tortillas

YIELD: 8 TORTILLAS

There is no comparison between homemade and store-bought tortillas. And there's no need to be intimidated. They are simple and divine. Serve them with tacos, fajitas, Turkey Picadillo (page 64), or just a smooth spread of butter. They're delightful and gluten-free!

1½ cups (155 grams) gluten-free masa harina
¼ teaspoon sea salt
1 cup (235 ml) warm water

Combine the masa harina and salt in a medium bowl. Add enough warm water to make a soft and pliable dough. Dough should be tender, not sticky or dry. Cover the bowl with a moist paper towel to keep the dough from drying.

Preheat griddle or skillet. Cut down the sides of a gallon-size (4 L) zip-top bag, leaving the bottom seam intact. Divide the dough into 3-inch (7.5 cm) balls, covering the remaining dough to keep from drying.

Unfold the bag and place a ball of dough between the sides of the bag; close. (Keep remaining balls covered with the moist paper towel.) Flatten dough to $\frac{1}{8}$-inch thickness with a tortilla press or a rolling pin. Place the flattened dough onto the griddle and cook for 45 seconds on each side. Remove and keep warm. Repeat with remaining balls of dough.

✳ FAST & SIMPLE SUGGESTION ✳

If you find you enjoy these easy, fresh, homemade tortillas, invest in an inexpensive tortilla press. It is an aluminum levered gadget that makes the process even simpler.

✳ RECIPE TIP: AVOID SUBSTITUTES ✳

Masa harina is the flour used to make traditional tortillas, tamales, and other Mexican dishes. It is made by grinding dried corn and then soaking the cornmeal in a lime solution. Cornmeal and corn flour cannot be substituted for masa harina. Be sure to confirm that the masa harina you find is gluten-free and not processed in a facility with wheat.

Butter Rolls

Quick, easy, heavenly, buttery dinner rolls in less than 30 minutes. I know it sounds too good to be true. But here you go. You can thank me later.

2 teaspoons (5 g) golden flaxseed meal
4 teaspoons (20 ml) very hot water
1 cup (140 grams) Kumquat's Gluten-Free All-Purpose Flour Blend (page 15) or gluten-free all-purpose flour
½ teaspoon baking soda
½ teaspoon baking powder
¼ teaspoon salt
½ cup (115 g) sour cream
½ cup (1 stick, or 112 g) butter, melted
1 tablespoon (15 ml) milk or milk alternative
Cooking spray

Preheat oven to 400°F (200°C, or gas mark 6).

Combine the flaxseed meal and hot water and stir until thick; set aside.

Combine the flour, baking soda, baking powder, and salt in a bowl. Mix in the flax slurry, sour cream, melted butter, and milk; stir until smooth. Spoon heaping tablespoonfuls (15 g) of batter into mini-muffin tins coated with cooking spray. (Fill any unused tins each with a teaspoon of water.) Bake for 17 minutes or until golden.

Cheddar-Dill Biscuits

These easy, cheesy biscuits are a perfect savory pairing with a fall soup. Flakey and tender, they're everything you remember biscuits to be from your gluten-eating days and more.

2 teaspoons (4.7 g) golden flaxseed meal

4 teaspoons (20 ml) very hot water

3 cups (about 390 grams) Kumquat's Gluten-Free All-Purpose Flour Blend (page 15) or gluten-free all-purpose flour

1 teaspoon sugar

1 tablespoon (14 g) baking powder

1 teaspoon baking soda

½ teaspoon salt

⅓ cup (75 g) cold butter, cut into small pieces

1 cup (235 ml) buttermilk

1½ cups (173 g) shredded extra-sharp Cheddar cheese

1½ tablespoons (6 g) chopped fresh dill

Cooking spray

Melted butter, for brushing

Preheat oven to 425°F (220°C, or gas mark 7).

Combine the flaxseed meal and hot water and stir until thick; set aside.

Combine the flour, sugar, baking powder, baking soda, and salt in a bowl. Cut in the cold butter with a pastry cutter or your fingers until the mixture resembles coarse meal. Add the buttermilk and flax slurry to the dry ingredients and stir well to combine. Stir in the cheese and dill.

Turn dough out onto a floured surface, and knead until well combined. Roll or pat into a 1-inch (2 cm) thickness, and then cut with a 2½-inch (6.4 cm) biscuit cutter. Place the biscuits close together on a baking sheet coated with cooking spray. Brush them with melted butter, and bake for 14 minutes or until golden.

✳ RECIPE TIP: D.I.Y. BUTTERMILK ✳

If you don't have buttermilk on hand, add one tablespoon (15 ml) apple cider or white vinegar to 1 cup (235 ml) milk. This method also works when using dairy-free milk, such as almond, rice, and coconut milks.

Honey Skillet Cornbread

YIELD: 8 TO 10 SERVINGS

Skillet cornbread is a staple at my house. Served alongside Red Beans & Rice with Andouille Sausage (page 80), Chocolate Chili (page 89), or merely a slab of butter and a drizzle of molasses, this recipe is always a hit. If you are sensitive to eggs, this one can be made without egg and is just as delicious.

⅓ cup (75 ml) canola oil
1 teaspoon golden flaxseed meal
2 teaspoons (10 ml) very hot water
1 cup (140 grams) Kumquat's Gluten-Free All-Purpose Flour Blend (page 15) or gluten-free all-purpose flour
1 cup (130 grams) gluten-free yellow cornmeal
2 tablespoons (26 g) sugar
1 tablespoon (14 g) baking powder
1 teaspoon salt
1 cup (235 ml) milk or milk alternative
¼ cup (85 g) honey
2 large eggs

Preheat oven to 450°F (230°C, or gas mark 8).

Pour the oil into a 10-inch (25 cm) ovenproof skillet. Place in the oven for 3 minutes as it preheats.

Combine the flaxseed meal and hot water and stir until thick; set aside.

Combine the flour, cornmeal, sugar, baking powder, and salt in a bowl. Combine the milk, honey, and eggs in a separate bowl or measuring cup. Add the milk mixture and flax slurry to the flour mixture and stir until combined.

Carefully remove the hot skillet from the oven. Pour batter into the skillet—it will bubble in the hot oil. Return the skillet to the oven and bake for 15 minutes until golden.

✳ FAST & SIMPLE SUGGESTION ✳

When measuring honey, it is helpful to first spray the measuring cup with cooking spray. The honey will then slide effortlessly right out of the cup.

Sweet Orange Biscuits

YIELD: ABOUT 11 BISCUITS

These beautiful biscuits are a perfect addition to any Sunday brunch. The citrusy sweetness and light texture are everything you'd hope for in a sweet biscuit. I love these.

FOR BISCUITS:
2 teaspoons (5 g) golden
   flaxseed meal
4 teaspoons (20 ml) very hot water
3 cups (about 390 grams) Kumquat's
   Gluten-Free All-Purpose Flour
   Blend (page 15) or gluten-free
   all-purpose flour
2 tablespoons (26 g) sugar
1 tablespoon (14 g) baking powder
1 teaspoon baking soda
½ teaspoon salt
⅓ cup (75 g) cold butter, cut into small
   pieces
1 tablespoon (6 g) organic orange zest
¾ cup (175 ml) buttermilk
¼ cup (60 ml) fresh orange juice
Cooking spray

FOR GLAZE:
1½ cups (180 g) powdered sugar
3½ tablespoons (53 ml) fresh orange
   juice
1 teaspoon organic orange zest

To make the biscuits: Preheat oven to 425°F (220°C, or gas mark 7).

Combine the flaxseed meal and hot water and stir until thick; set aside.

Combine the flour, sugar, baking powder, baking soda, and salt in a bowl. Cut in the butter with a pastry cutter or your fingers until the mixture resembles coarse meal. Stir in 1 tablespoon (6 g) orange zest. Combine the buttermilk and orange juice. Add the buttermilk mixture and flax slurry to the dry ingredients and stir well to combine.

Turn the dough out onto a well-floured surface; knead until well combined. Roll or pat into a 1-inch (2.5 cm) thickness, and then cut with a 2½-inch (6.4 cm) biscuit cutter. Place the biscuits close together on a baking sheet coated with cooking spray. Bake for 14 minutes or until golden.

To make the glaze: Meanwhile, combine the powdered sugar, orange juice, and 1 teaspoon orange zest in a medium bowl.

Allow biscuits to cool and then spread icing evenly over top of the biscuits.

✳ RECIPE TIP: CHOOSE ORGANIC CITRUS ✳

When zesting, grating, or using the whole fruit, always use organic citrus. Pesticides and sprays remain on the skins of the fruits, so when the peel will be removed and discarded and only the segments of the fruit eaten, it's not quite as important to choose organic. When using both the zest and juice of a citrus fruit, always zest first.

Pâte Brisée

YIELD: 2 (9-INCH, OR 23 CM) CRUSTS (enough for 1 double-crust pie, 1 lattice-topped pie, or 2 single-crust pies)

Pâte Brisée is a fancy French name for a flakey crust used to make savory and sweet pies. Easy and gluten-free, the possibilities are limitless!

2½ cups (350 grams) Kumquat's Gluten-Free All-Purpose Flour Blend (page 15) or gluten-free all-purpose flour

¾ teaspoon salt

1 cup (2 sticks, or 225 g) unsalted butter

⅓ to ½ cup (75 to 120 ml) ice water

Pulse the flour and salt in the container of a food processor. Add the butter and pulse until the mixture resembles coarse meal. Gradually blend in enough ice water to form moist clumps. Gather dough into a ball and divide in half. Form dough into 2 balls and then flatten into disks. Wrap each disk in plastic and chill until ready to use.

Pâte Sucrée

YIELD: 2 (9-INCH, OR 23 CM) CRUSTS (enough for 1 double-crust pie, 1 lattice-topped pie, or 2 single-crust pies)

Pâte Sucrée is a fancy French name for the flakey crust used to make sweet pies. The difference between this recipe and Pâte Brisée is the little bit of added sugar. Use this crust for pies, tarts, and galettes.

2½ cups (350 grams) Kumquat's Gluten-Free All-Purpose Flour Blend (page 15) or gluten-free all-purpose flour

2 tablespoons (26 g) sugar

¾ teaspoon salt

1 cup (2 sticks, or 225 g) unsalted butter

⅓ to ½ cup (75 to 120 ml) ice water

Pulse the flour, sugar, and salt in the container of a food processor. Add the butter and pulse until the mixture resembles coarse meal. Gradually blend in enough ice water to form moist clumps. Gather dough into a ball and divide in half. Form dough into 2 balls and then flatten into disks. Wrap each disk in plastic and chill until ready to use.

✳ RECIPE TIP: FREEZE FOR THE FUTURE ✳

Pâte Sucrée and Pâte Brisée can be wrapped tightly with plastic wrap, placed in a plastic freezer bag, and frozen for up to 2 months.

Pepper-Parmesan Biscuits

YIELD: ABOUT 11 BISCUITS

These biscuits are one of my favorites. Flakey, rich, and cheesy with just a bit of a kick from the black pepper, they're a perfect partner to a savory soup.

2 teaspoons (5 g) golden flaxseed meal
4 teaspoons (20 ml) very hot water
2 cups (about 280 grams) Kumquat's
  Gluten-Free All-Purpose Flour
  Blend (page 15) or gluten-free
  all-purpose flour
1 tablespoon (14 g) baking powder
1 teaspoon freshly ground black pepper
½ teaspoon salt
½ cup (1 stick, or 112 g) cold butter, cut
  into small pieces
¾ cup (60 g) shredded Parmesan
  cheese
1 cup (235 ml) heavy cream
Cooking spray
Melted butter for brushing

Preheat oven to 450°F (230°C, or gas mark 8).

Combine the flaxseed meal and hot water and stir until thick; set aside.

Combine the flour, baking powder, pepper, and salt in a bowl. Cut in the butter with a pastry cutter or your fingers until the mixture resembles coarse meal. Stir in the Parmesan cheese. Add the heavy cream and flax slurry to the dry ingredients and stir well to combine.

Turn dough out onto a clean surface; knead until well combined. Roll or press into a 1-inch (2.5 cm) thickness and then cut with a 2½-inch (6.4 cm) biscuit cutter. Place the biscuits close together on a baking sheet coated with cooking spray. Brush with melted butter. Bake for 15 minutes or until golden.

✳ RECIPE TIP: CHILL FOR EXTENDED SHELF LIFE ✳

When blending your own flours, store your Kumquat's Gluten-Free All-Purpose Flour Blend (page 15) in your refrigerator. Store excess, unblended flours in your freezer for their longest shelf-life and to keep the oils in the flours from becoming rancid.

8

Sweet Treats in a Hurry

IF YOU WERE TO ASK ANYONE WHO KNOWS ME, or if you've been to my blog, you would find that sweets are kind of my thing. Of course my dietitian side must temper my unbridled sweet tooth, but I do love an occasional sweet treat. Therefore, this chapter is right up my alley. Some of these recipes require my Kumquat's Gluten-Free All-Purpose Flour Blend (page 15) or your favorite gluten-free all-purpose flour. But some of the recipes are just naturally gluten-free for those families who don't want to invest in gluten-free flours when entertaining gluten-free friends. Get ready to go to your happy place. . . .

Bananas with Caramel-Chocolate Sauce

YIELD: 4 (4-OUNCE, OR 125 G) SERVINGS

These are the ultimate in ooey, gooey, sticky deliciousness. These bananas are sinfully good served over cake or ice cream or just all by their scrumptious selves.

¼ cup (55 g) butter
½ cup (100 g) sugar
½ cup (120 ml) heavy cream
½ teaspoon vanilla extract
⅛ teaspoon salt
4 peeled, sliced bananas
⅓ cup (58 g) chocolate chips

Melt the butter in a large skillet over medium heat. Stir in the sugar and cook, stirring constantly, until the sugar melts and becomes golden brown. Stir in the cream, vanilla, and salt (mixture will bubble and may harden a bit). Cook for 1 minute, or until the mixture liquefies and thickens. Stir in the bananas, and cook for 1 minute. Stir in the chocolate chips. Serve immediately.

Cinnamon-Almond Cookies

YIELD: 1 DOZEN COOKIES

My mother-in-law declared these nutty, chewy, grain-free treats her favorite cookies ever. I love how they really couldn't be easier and are ready in a flash. That little hint of saltiness and sweetness lingers with each bite. So yummy . . .

1 cup (145 g) roasted, salted almonds
¾ cup (150 g) sugar
½ teaspoon cinnamon
½ teaspoon vanilla extract
1 large egg
Cooking spray

Preheat oven to 325°F (170°C, or gas mark 3).

Pulse the almonds in a food processor until they form a very fine powder-like meal. (Be careful not to make almond butter.) Transfer the almonds to a medium bowl and stir in the sugar, cinnamon, vanilla, and egg.

Line 2 baking sheets with parchment paper. Lightly spray hands with cooking spray. Roll 1 heaping tablespoon (15 g) of the mixture into a ball and flatten to ½-inch (12 mm) thickness on prepared baking sheets, leaving room for cookies to spread. Repeat with the remaining mixture. Bake for 20 minutes or until golden. Cool slightly on wire rack.

Coffee-Chip Ice Cream

This is truly the simplest approach to heavenly, handmade, fresh ice cream . . . and all in 15 minutes or less. If you're a coffee addict, like a few of us in my family, this quick and delectable treat will definitely make your short list of go-to desserts.

2 tablespoons (26 g) sugar
1 cup (235 ml) heavy cream or coconut milk beverage, such as So Delicious
1 tablespoon (5 g) instant espresso powder (decaffeinated, if desired)
2 tablespoons (22 g) miniature chocolate chips
½ cup (150 g) coarse salt
Ice

Combine the sugar, cream or coconut milk, instant espresso powder, and chocolate chips in a quart-size (1 L) resealable plastic bag; seal tightly. Place the bag inside of a gallon-size (4 L) resealable plastic bag. Fill the remaining space in the outer gallon-size bag with the salt and enough ice to fill the outer bag without stuffing it; seal tightly. Shake and massage the bag for 5 to 10 minutes or until the mixture freezes to the desired consistency. (The bag will be cold and wet; wrap it in a towel, if desired.) Scoop ice cream from the inner bag and serve immediately. Store in the freezer, if you do not eat it all in one sitting!

✴ RECIPE TIP: MAKE IT KID FRIENDLY ✴

Omit the espresso powder and this ice cream is a fabulous one to make with kids. Put those little arms to work to burn some endless energy, teach them a little food science, and then reward them with a sweet treat made by their own hands. Feel free to throw in ¼ cup (55 g) of your favorite fruit or nuts. If you're feeling especially decadent, serve this on top of the Chocolate-Chunk Skillet Cookie on page 129 or the Triple Chocolate Truffle Brownies on page 164.

Chocolate-Chunk Skillet Cookie

YIELD: 4 TO 6 (3-OUNCE, OR 84 G) SERVINGS

If you're a fan of warm, gooey, fresh-out-of-the-oven cookies with oozy pools of chocolate, then this one's for you. This one-pan favorite is best served topped with melty vanilla ice cream. Grab some spoons and dig on in.

½ cup (1 stick, or 112 g) butter
¾ cup (170 g) packed brown sugar
½ cup (100 g) sugar
1 teaspoon vanilla extract
1 large egg or ¼ cup (60 ml) egg substitute
1½ cups (210 grams) Kumquat's Gluten-Free All-Purpose Flour Blend (page 15) or gluten-free all-purpose flour
½ teaspoon baking soda
½ teaspoon salt
1¼ cups (219 g) semi-sweet chocolate chunks
Vanilla ice cream, for serving

Preheat oven to 350°F (180°C, or gas mark 4).

Melt the butter in an 8-inch (20 cm) ovenproof skillet over medium heat. Remove from heat. Stir in the brown sugar, sugar, and vanilla until combined. Add the egg or egg substitute and stir to combine. Add the flour, baking soda, and salt and stir until smooth. Fold in the chocolate chunks.

Bake for 25 minutes or to desired degree of doneness. Serve with vanilla ice cream.

✳ DID YOU KNOW? ✳

Some chocolate bars, chunks, and chips are manufactured in facilities that also process wheat and gluten products. Be certain the chocolates you buy are gluten-free.

Chocolate-Dunked Macaroons

YIELD: ABOUT 1½ DOZEN
MACAROONS

Crisp and crunchy on the outside with a chewy, soft center, these effortless and beautiful coconut cookies are one of my favorites . . . and naturally gluten-free!

3 large egg whites
¾ cup (150 g) sugar
½ teaspoon vanilla extract
3 cups (255 g) unsweetened coconut flakes
Cooking spray
6 ounces (171 g) bittersweet (60 percent cacao) chocolate, finely chopped

Preheat oven to 350°F (180°C, or gas mark 4).

Combine the egg whites, sugar, vanilla, and coconut in a medium bowl and stir well to combine. Lightly spray hands with cooking spray. Roll 1 heaping tablespoon (15 g) of the mixture into a ball and flatten to 1-inch (2.5 cm) thickness on a parchment-lined baking sheet. Repeat with the remaining mixture. Bake for 15 to 17 minutes or until just golden. Transfer to rack to cool.

Meanwhile, heat the chocolate in the microwave on HIGH in 30-second intervals, stirring well in between, until melted. Dip the bottoms of the macaroons in the chocolate and return to the parchment. Chill for 1 to 2 minutes to set.

No-Bake Chocolate-Peanut Butter Cookies

YIELD: ABOUT 1 DOZEN
COOKIES

I dare you to find a tastier cookie that is this easy! They're chewy, chocolaty, and fast!

1 cup (85 grams) gluten-free rolled oats
½ cup (13 g) gluten-free crisped rice cereal
¼ cup (21 g) shredded, sweetened coconut
½ cup (88 g) chocolate chips
¼ cup (65 g) peanut butter
¼ cup (60 ml) canned unsweetened coconut milk
⅛ teaspoon salt

Combine the oats, rice cereal, and coconut in a large bowl.

Combine the chocolate chips, peanut butter coconut milk, and salt in a medium saucepan. Heat over medium heat until the chocolate melts and the mixture is well combined.

Pour the chocolate mixture over the oat mixture, and stir to combine. Spoon 1 heaping tablespoon (15 g) of the mixture onto a baking sheet lined with parchment paper. Repeat with remaining dough. Chill the cookies on the baking sheet for 15 to 20 minutes or until set.

Peppermint-Chocolate Crinkles

YIELD: ABOUT 1 DOZEN COOKIES

These soft, fudgy cookies are rolled in powdered sugar before they are baked and begin to look crinkled in the oven. Finely crushed peppermints make them a delightful holiday cookie or a perfect all-year treat for a mint-chocolate lover like me.

¾ cup (about 105 grams) Kumquat's Gluten-Free All-Purpose Flour Blend (page 15) or gluten-free all-purpose flour

⅓ cup (43 g) cocoa powder

¾ teaspoon baking powder

¼ teaspoon salt

3 tablespoons (42 g) butter, softened

½ cup (115 g) packed brown sugar

1 large egg

⅓ cup (95 g) finely crushed peppermint candies (about 20 round peppermints)

2 tablespoons (7.5 g) powdered sugar

Preheat oven to 400°F (200°C, or gas mark 6).

Combine the flour, cocoa powder, baking powder, and salt in a medium bowl.

Cream the butter and brown sugar in a large bowl with an electric mixer for 3 minutes. Beat in the egg. Add the flour mixture and crushed peppermints to the butter mixture and stir until well combined.

Roll 1 heaping tablespoon (15 g) of dough into a ball. Roll the ball in the powdered sugar and place on a parchment-lined baking sheet, spacing them 2 inches (5 cm) apart. Bake for 13 minutes or until the sides of the cookies are firm and the tops are cracked. Cool on a rack.

> ✷ FAST & SIMPLE SUGGESTION ✷
>
> To finely crush peppermints, place the candies in a zip-top plastic bag and pound them with a rolling pin or the flat side of a meat mallet. It's fast and mess-free!

Fruit & Nut Bark

YIELD: 8 (2-OUNCE, OR 57 G) SERVINGS

Barks are a sweet, chocolaty ending to any meal. I've topped this beautiful bark with nuts and dried fruits for a naturally delicious flavor combination. If you're feeling especially generous, it would also make a gorgeous gift.

12 ounces (342 g) dark chocolate
   (60 percent cacao), chopped, divided
½ cup (60 g) dried cranberries
⅓ cup (41 g) chopped pistachios
⅓ cup (43 g) chopped dried apricots
¼ cup (28 g) slivered almonds
2 teaspoons (4 g) fresh organic
   orange zest

Heat 8 ounces (228 g) chopped chocolate in the microwave on HIGH for 30 seconds; stir well. Heat chocolate on HIGH 30 additional seconds; stir well. If not completely melted, heat an additional 15 seconds; stir well. Stir in the remaining chopped chocolate and stir until melted and combined. Pour the melted chocolate onto a baking sheet lined with parchment paper and spread the mixture into a rectangle that is ¼-inch (6 mm) thick. Working quickly, sprinkle the cranberries, pistachios, apricots, almonds, and orange zest evenly over the chocolate.

Place the baking sheet in the refrigerator for 7 to 10 minutes to harden. Break or cut the chocolate into pieces.

✳ DID YOU KNOW? ✳

Some chocolate bars, chunks, and chips are manufactured in facilities that also process wheat and gluten products. Be certain the chocolates you buy are gluten-free.

132   FAST & SIMPLE GLUTEN-FREE

Gingersnap Cookies with White Chocolate

These are one of my all-time favorite holiday cookies (and happen to be my husband's favorite cookies of all time.) They are the perfect combination of chewy, crunchy, and spicy, and they make me happy.

1 teaspoon golden flaxseed meal

2 teaspoons (10 ml) very hot water

2 cups (280 grams) Kumquat's Gluten-Free All-Purpose Flour Blend (page 15) or gluten-free all-purpose flour

2 teaspoons (9 g) baking soda

2 teaspoons (4 g) ground ginger

1 teaspoon cinnamon

½ teaspoon salt

⅛ teaspoon ground cloves

¾ cup (175 ml) oil

1 cup (200 g) plus ¼ cup (50 g) sugar, divided

1 large egg

¼ cup (85 g) molasses

2 ounces (57 g) white chocolate, chopped

Preheat oven to 350°F (180°C, or gas mark 4).

Line 2 baking sheets with parchment paper. Combine the flaxseed meal and hot water in a small bowl. Stir until a thick slurry forms and set aside.

Combine the flour, baking soda, ginger, cinnamon, salt, and cloves in a large bowl. Combine the oil and 1 cup (200 g) sugar in another large bowl and beat with an electric mixer for 2 minutes or until pale in color. Beat in the egg and molasses. Add the flour mixture to the oil mixture and stir until well combined.

Roll 2 tablespoonfuls (28 g) of dough into a ball (a little smaller than a golf ball). Roll dough ball in remaining sugar to coat. Place on baking sheet and repeat with remaining dough, placing balls 2 inches (5 cm) apart on parchment. Bake both baking sheets for 12 to 14 minutes or until the edges are browned and the tops are crackled. Transfer the cookies to a rack to cool.

While the cookies bake, carefully heat the white chocolate in the top of a double boiler over simmering water or in a microwave until melted. Drizzle the chocolate evenly over slightly cooled cookies. Refrigerate the cookies for a couple of minutes to set the chocolate, if desired.

✳ FAST & SIMPLE SUGGESTION ✳

When measuring molasses, spray your measuring cup with cooking spray and it will easily slide out into your bowl.

Peanut Butter & Chocolate Crispy Squares

YIELD: 9 TO 12 SQUARES

Two things that make my sweet tooth happy are marshmallow-crispy squares and chocolate–peanut butter cups. These squares are the best of both worlds.

1 package (10 ounces, or 283 g) miniature marshmallows
3 tablespoons (42 g) butter
6 cups (156 g) gluten-free crisped rice cereal
Cooking spray
¼ cup (65 g) creamy peanut butter
6 ounces (171 g) dark chocolate, chopped, divided

Melt the marshmallows and butter in a large saucepan over medium heat, stirring frequently. Allow to brown a little, but not burn. Carefully and quickly stir in the cereal; stir to coat. Press into a 9-inch (23 cm) baking pan coated with cooking spray.

Heat the peanut butter and 4 ounces (228 g) chocolate in the microwave on HIGH for 30 seconds; stir well. Heat an additional 30 seconds; stir well. Stir in remaining chopped chocolate; stir until melted and smooth.

Spread the chocolate mixture evenly over the top of the cereal in the pan. Freeze for 10 minutes or until the chocolate sets. Cut into squares and serve.

Peaches Foster

YIELD: 6 (4-OUNCE, OR 114 G) SERVINGS

A divine marriage of two classics, peaches and cream, and Bananas Foster, this heavenly dessert will not leave you disappointed. It's a quick and easy way to use ripe and ready peaches during peach season. Plus, whose inner child doesn't love the flame of a flambé?

3 tablespoons (42 g) butter
⅓ cup (75 g) packed brown sugar
1 teaspoon vanilla extract
½ teaspoon cinnamon
1 pound (455 g) peeled, sliced fresh peaches or thawed frozen
¼ cup (60 ml) dark rum
3 cups (420 g) vanilla ice cream, divided, for serving

Melt the butter in a large skillet over medium heat. Stir in the brown sugar, vanilla, and cinnamon and cook for 2 minutes. Add the peaches and cook for 3 minutes or until tender. Remove the pan from the heat. Add the rum to the pan and ignite the rum with a long match or torch. Carefully and gently stir the peaches until the flame disappears. Serve peach mixture over ½ cup (70 g) servings of ice cream.

Pear Dutch Baby

Also called a "German pancake," this baby is a baked pancake served for either a sweet breakfast or dessert. Because of all the eggs in the batter, the pancake rises to a beautiful golden bouffant puff in the oven and falls when cooling.

5 tablespoons (70 g) butter

2 pears, peeled, cored and sliced into ¼-inch wedges

1 tablespoon (15 g) packed brown sugar

1 teaspoon fresh lemon juice

¼ teaspoon cinnamon

½ cup (120 ml) milk or milk alternative

½ cup (70 grams) Kumquat's Gluten-Free All-Purpose Flour Blend (page 15) or gluten-free all-purpose flour

4 large eggs

2 tablespoons (26 g) sugar

½ teaspoon vanilla extract

¼ teaspoon salt

Powdered sugar, for dusting

Preheat oven to 450°F (230°C, or gas mark 8).

Melt the butter in a large ovenproof skillet over medium-high heat. Transfer 2 tablespoons (30 ml) butter to the the blender container. Add the pears, brown sugar, lemon juice, and cinnamon to the skillet. Cook for 3 minutes or until the pears begin to soften.

Meanwhile, add the milk, flour, eggs, sugar, vanilla, and salt to the butter in the blender. Blend until smooth. Pour the batter over the pears and transfer the skillet to the oven. Bake for 15 minutes or until the pancake is puffed and golden. Dust with powdered sugar, if desired, and serve immediately.

CHAPTER 9

Extra-Time-to-Bake Goodies

IF YOU HAVE A LITTLE TIME, THEN IT'S TIME. Time to preheat the oven, throw on your apron, and reclaim your inner baker in your own gluten-free kitchen. And no need to be shy; all of these recipes are quite simple to prepare. They just take a little more time baking in the oven or chilling in the fridge than the rest of the recipes in this book. But not to worry . . . that extra time is "inactive time," so you can get back to doing all of the other things that the day requires.

Kumquat's Pizza Dough

YIELD: 1 (16-INCH, OR 40 CM) PIZZA CRUST

I don't know about you, but I got tired of hard, flat, crunchy gluten-free pizza dough really fast. I'm happy to say, "Welcome back, delicious pizza dough!" This recipe makes a thick and chewy and soft, yeast-flavored dough that bakes into a gorgeous 16-inch (40 cm) pizza. Reclaim your pizza!

1½ tablespoons (10.5 g) golden flaxseed meal

3 tablespoons (45 ml) very hot water

3 cups (420 grams) Kumquat's Gluten-Free All-Purpose Flour Blend (page 15) or gluten-free all-purpose flour

2 teaspoons (12 g) salt

5 teaspoons (20 g) active dry yeast

⅓ cup (75 ml) olive oil

1 tablespoon (13 g) sugar

1 cup (235 ml) warm water (110°F, or 43°C), divided

Olive oil for brushing

½ teaspoon garlic powder

Combine the flaxseed meal and 3 tablespoons (45 ml) very hot water in a small bowl until a slurry is formed; set aside.

Combine the flour and salt in a large mixing bowl or bowl of a stand mixer. Combine the yeast, olive oil, sugar, and ½ cup (120 ml) warm water in a medium bowl or measuring cup. Allow to rest for 3 minutes for yeast to activate.

Add the yeast mixture to the flour mixture and mix for 1 minute. Add the flax slurry to the dough and mix until the dough comes together in a ball, about 5 to 7 minutes. (If dough is too dry, add warm water a teaspoon at a time to form a tender, pliable dough.) Set the dough aside, cover, and allow to rest for 1 hour.

To prebake the crust, preheat oven to 450°F (230°C, or gas mark 8).

Roll the dough between 2 pieces of parchment paper to desired thickness. Transfer the dough to a pizza stone or baking sheet. Brush the entire dough with olive oil and sprinkle evenly with the garlic powder. Top with favorite, fresh ingredients and bake 16 minutes or until cheese is melted and crust is cooked.

EXTRA-TIME-TO-BAKE GOODIES   141

Berry Oat Scones

I've always been a sucker for a good scone. They combine the butter of a biscuit with the sugar of a muffin to make baked perfection. This one is a sweet way to take advantage of fresh berries in the early summer and includes oats for added texture.

1½ cups (150 grams) gluten-free rolled oats

1⅓ cups (190 grams) Kumquat's Gluten-Free All-Purpose Flour Blend (page 15) or gluten-free all-purpose flour

⅓ cup (75 g) packed dark brown sugar

1 tablespoon (14 g) baking powder

4 teaspoons (9 g) golden flaxseed meal

½ teaspoon cinnamon

½ teaspoon salt

½ cup (1 stick, or 112 g) chilled butter

½ cup (120 ml) heavy cream

1 large egg

1 large egg yolk

½ cup (75 g) fresh blueberries

½ cup (65 g) fresh raspberries

Cooking spray

2 tablespoons (28 g) turbinado sugar, for sprinkling

Preheat oven to 400°F (200°C, or gas mark 6).

Combine the oats, flour, brown sugar, baking powder, flaxseed meal, cinnamon, and salt in a large bowl. Cut the butter into the flour mixture with a pastry blender or with your fingers until the mixture resembles coarse meal.

Combine the cream, egg, and egg yolk in a medium bowl or measuring cup. Add the cream mixture to the dry ingredients and stir until combined. Add the berries and gently stir to combine.

Using very lightly floured hands, form dough into an 8-inch (20 cm) circle on a baking sheet coated with cooking spray. Freeze the dough for 10 minutes.

Cut the dough into 8 wedges with a sharp knife or pastry scraper and separate each out slightly. You want to leave a couple inches (5 cm) of space between each for any spreading while baking. Sprinkle with the turbinado sugar. Bake for 18 to 20 minutes or until golden brown.

✳ FAST & SIMPLE SUGGESTION ✳

When using flax as a binder, it is possible to buy the whole seeds and grind them yourself, but I recommend buying flaxseed meal if you can, as the little seeds are already ground and ready to go! Just store them in the refrigerator to keep from going rancid.

Homemade Blueberry Pop Tarts

YIELD: 9 TARTS

Everyone deserves a pop tart. And now they can be back in your gluten-free life just as easy as pie. These are not the overprocessed, dense tarts from the grocery store shelves, so rewarm them in the oven instead of the toaster.

1 recipe Pâte Sucrée (page 122) or gluten-free pastry dough, softened
1 large egg, lightly beaten
1 cup (about 8 ounces, or 320 g) blueberry jam
Milk, for brushing
Turbinado sugar, for sprinkling

Preheat oven to 400°F (200°C, or gas mark 6).

Roll half the Pâte Sucrée to ⅛-inch thickness between two lightly floured pieces of parchment paper into a 15 × 9-inch (38 × 23 cm) rectangle. Repeat with remaining dough. Cut each rectangle of dough into nine (3 × 5-inch, or 7.5 × 13 cm) rectangles, yielding a total of 18 rectangles.

Brush the tops of 9 rectangles with the egg. Top each egg-brushed rectangle with a heaping tablespoon (20 g) of jam and spread (12 mm) over all but a ½-inch (12 mm) border around the edges. Place a second rectangle on top of the jam and press firmly around the edges to seal dough well. Press edges of the tart with the tines of a fork. Repeat with remaining tarts.

Place the tarts on a large jelly-roll pan or baking sheet lined with parchment paper. Prick the tops of the tarts multiple times with a fork or a toothpick. Brush the tops of the tarts with milk and sprinkle with the turbinado sugar. Bake for 16 minutes or until golden. Allow to cool.

✸ RECIPE TIP: FROST AWAY! ✸

I'm the type that doesn't think a Pop Tart is even quite worth it if it doesn't have a colorful frosting. If you're like me, stir 2 teaspoons (10 ml) milk and 1 teaspoon blueberry jam into ⅓ cup (80 g) powdered sugar. Spread the mixture over cooled tarts and give your inner child a big hug.

Caramel Apple Galettes

My favorite fall fair flavors come together easily to make these rustic, free-form, irresistible tarts.

3 small Granny Smith apples (about 13 ounces, or 368 g), peeled and sliced into ¼-inch slices

½ cup (115 g) packed brown sugar

2 tablespoons (16 g) Kumquat's Gluten-Free All-Purpose Flour Blend (page 15) or gluten-free all-purpose flour

2 teaspoons (10 ml) lemon juice

2 teaspoons (10 ml) vanilla extract

½ teaspoon cinnamon

¼ teaspoon salt

½ recipe Pâte Sucrée (page 122)

1 large egg, lightly beaten

1 tablespoon (14 g) turbinado sugar

½ cup (164 g) gluten-free caramel topping, for serving

Preheat oven to 425°F (220°C, or gas mark 7). Line a baking sheet with parchment paper.

Combine the apples, brown sugar, flour, lemon juice, vanilla, cinnamon, and salt in a medium bowl.

Divide the dough into 4 pieces. Roll 1 piece of dough into a 7-inch (18 cm) circle between 2 pieces of parchment paper or waxed paper. Carefully peel off the parchment and place the dough circle on the parchment-lined baking sheet. Place ¼ of the apple mixture in the center of the dough circle, leaving a 2-inch (5 cm) border. Fold the edges of the dough inward toward the center, pressing gently to seal; pinch together any cracks in the tender dough. The dough will only partially cover the apples. Repeat with remaining dough and apples.

Brush the dough with egg and sprinkle with the turbinado sugar.

Bake for 20 minutes or until the pastry is cooked and lightly browned. Drizzle galettes with caramel topping.

146   FAST & SIMPLE GLUTEN-FREE

Flourless Chocolate Mini-Cakes with Praline Sauce

YIELD: 12 SERVINGS

There's nothing like the truffle-like texture and chocolaty mouthful of a flourless cake. And because these are small, you don't have to worry about portion control, other than resisting the urge to go back for another. Top it all off with the South's generous contribution to the world of candy, the praline, in sauce version.

FOR MINI-CAKES:

⅓ cup (37 g) chopped pecans
3 large eggs, separated
1¼ cups (250 g) sugar
2 tablespoons (28 g) unsweetened cocoa
4 ounces (114 g) bittersweet chocolate, coarsely chopped
3 tablespoons (45 ml) warm water
Cooking spray

FOR PRALINE SAUCE:

1 cup (150 g) packed brown sugar
½ cup (120 ml) evaporated milk
1 tablespoon (14 g) butter
½ cup (55 g) chopped pecans
½ teaspoon vanilla extract

To make the cakes: Preheat oven to 425°F (220°C, or gas mark 7).

Pulse the ⅓ cup (37 g) pecans in a small food processor or blender just until pecans form a paste (about 1 minute), scraping down sides if necessary. Set aside.

Combine the egg yolks, sugar, and cocoa in a large bowl. Melt the chocolate in the microwave for 45 seconds on HIGH, stirring every 15 seconds. Set aside.

Beat the egg whites in a large bowl on high speed with an electric mixer until stiff peaks form. Add the pecan paste, chocolate, and warm water to the egg yolk mixture. Stir until smooth. Gently fold in half the beaten egg whites and then fold in the remaining half. Spoon the mixture evenly into 12 muffin cups coated with cooking spray.

Bake for 10 minutes or until almost set but soft in the center. Place on a rack and cool 10 minutes.

To make the praline sauce: Meanwhile, combine the brown sugar, evaporated milk, and butter in a medium saucepan. Bring to a simmer over medium-high heat, stirring occasionally. Boil 1 minute or until sugar dissolves and the mixture thickens slightly. Remove from heat and stir in the pecans and vanilla. Let stand 10 minutes before serving.

Invert the cakes onto dessert plates and serve with Praline Sauce.

Lemon-Lime Cheesecake with Gingersnap Crust

YIELD: 12 SERVINGS

Citrus and gingersnaps are one of my favorite flavoring pairings. And because my husband is a huge cheesecake fan, this recipe was a hit with my whole family. It's as easy as cake and relatively foolproof.

FOR CRUST:
2 cups (231 g) crushed gluten-free gingersnaps (such as Mi-del), about 33 cookies
3 tablespoons (42 g) butter, melted

FOR CHEESECAKE:
1½ pounds (669 g) cream cheese, softened
1 cup (200 g) sugar
4 large eggs
¾ cup (173 g) sour cream
1 tablespoon (8 g) Kumquat's Gluten-Free All-Purpose Flour Blend (page 15) or gluten-free all-purpose flour
1 tablespoon (6 g) grated organic lemon zest
1 tablespoon (6 g) grated organic lime zest
2 tablespoons (30 ml) fresh lemon juice
2 tablespoons (30 ml) fresh lime juice

To make the crust: Preheat oven to 350°F (180°C, or gas mark 4).

Combine the crushed gingersnaps and butter in a medium bowl and mix until the crumbs are well coated with the butter. Firmly press the mixture into the bottom and up ½-inch (12 mm) on the sides of a 9-inch (23 cm) springform pan. Bake for 8 minutes. Remove from oven and then reduce oven to 300°F (150°C, or gas mark 2).

To make the cheesecake: Meanwhile, combine the cream cheese and sugar in a large bowl. Beat with an electric mixer for 3 minutes. Add the eggs one at a time, beating after each addition. Beat in the sour cream, flour, zests, and juices until just smooth. Pour the mixture into the baked crust.

Bake for 65 minutes or until the sides are cooked and the center barely jiggles when the cake is gently shaken. Run a thin-bladed knife between the cake and pan rim. Cool completely; cover and chill at least 3 hours or overnight. Remove the sides of the springform pan and serve.

> ✳ RECIPE TIP: PAT CRUST PERFECTLY ✳
>
> Place your hand in a plastic sandwich bag and press firmly on the gingersnap mixture to sufficiently form the crust in the pan.

Lemon-Poppy Seed Tea Bread

YIELD: 1 (8-INCH, OR 20 CM) LOAF

I love quick breads. They are just like muffins, but even less fussy, just as their name implies. This classic is delightfully lemony and would make a welcomed and lovely addition to a brunch or afternoon tea.

1¾ cups (240 grams) Kumquat's Gluten-Free All-Purpose Flour Blend (page 15) or gluten-free all-purpose flour
1 teaspoon baking powder
½ teaspoon salt
½ cup (120 ml) canola oil
¾ cup (150 g) sugar
2 large eggs
1½ teaspoons (7 g) vanilla extract
2 teaspoons (4 g) organic lemon zest
¾ cup (175 ml) milk or milk alternative
4 tablespoons (60 ml) fresh lemon juice, divided
3 tablespoons (23 g) poppy seeds
Cooking spray
1 cup (120 g) powdered sugar

Preheat oven to 350°F (180°C, or gas mark 4).

Combine the flour, baking powder, and salt in a large bowl.

In another large bowl, beat the oil and sugar with an electric mixer for 2 minutes. Add the eggs and vanilla and beat well. Stir in the lemon zest. Mix in the dry ingredients alternately with the milk, beginning and ending with the flour mixture. Stir in 2 tablespoons (30 ml) lemon juice and the poppy seeds. Pour the batter into an 8 × 4-inch (20 × 10 cm) loaf pan coated with cooking spray.

Bake for 50 minutes or until a wooden skewer or pick inserted in the center of the loaf comes out clean. Cool in the pan on a rack.

Meanwhile, combine the powdered sugar and remaining lemon juice in a small bowl or measuring cup. Pour the glaze evenly over the cooled loaf.

EXTRA-TIME-TO-BAKE GOODIES   153

Maple Oat Nut Scones

I used to love poring over the pastry case at the coffee shop, picking out precisely which treat I wanted to go with my coffee. Most every time it was a Maple Oat Nut Scone. Since I now know those gluten-filled goodies are no friends of my tummy, I took on the task of developing a gluten-free version. These are it exactly!

FOR GLAZED PECANS:
¾ cup (83 g) chopped pecans
3 tablespoons (39 g) sugar
¼ teaspoon cinnamon
2 teaspoons (10 ml) water

FOR SCONES:
4 teaspoons (28 g) golden flaxseed meal
4 teaspoons (20 ml) hot water
1½ cups (150 grams) gluten-free rolled oats, coarsely ground in a blender or food processor
1⅔ cups (190 grams) Kumquat's Gluten-Free All-Purpose Flour Blend (page 15) or gluten-free all-purpose flour
⅓ cup (75 g) packed dark brown sugar
1 tablespoon (14 g) baking powder
½ teaspoon cinnamon
½ teaspoon salt
½ cup (1 stick, or 112 g) cold butter, cut into small pieces
⅓ cup (75 ml) heavy cream
3 tablespoons (45 ml) Grade B maple syrup
1 large egg
1 large egg yolk
¾ teaspoon maple extract

FOR GLAZES:
1¾ cups (210 g) powdered sugar, divided
6½ teaspoons (32.5 ml) milk or milk alternative, divided
½ teaspoon maple extract

To make the glazed pecans: Combine the pecans, 3 tablespoons (39 g) sugar, ¼ teaspoon cinnamon, and water in a small skillet. Bring the mixture to a boil over medium-high heat; cook, stirring frequently, until sticky. Transfer the mixture to a piece of parchment or waxed paper. Spread to a single layer and set aside.

To make the scones: Combine the flaxseed meal and water; stir to make a paste. Set aside.

Combine the oats, flour, brown sugar, baking powder, ½ teaspoon cinnamon, and salt in a large bowl. Cut the butter into the flour mixture with a pastry blender or your fingers until the mixture resembles coarse meal.

Combine the cream, maple syrup, whole egg, egg yolk, and maple extract in a medium bowl or measuring cup. Add the cream mixture and the flax paste to the dry ingredients; stir until combined. Add the sugared pecans, breaking up large pieces if necessary; stir to combine.

Form the dough into an 8-inch (20 cm) circle on a parchment-lined baking sheet using very lightly floured hands. Chill the dough for 30 minutes.

Preheat oven to 400°F (200°C, or gas mark 6).

Cut the dough into 8 wedges, leaving room between the scones to spread while baking without touching. Bake for 18 to 20 minutes or until golden brown. Allow to cool completely on a wire rack.

To make the glazes: For maple glaze, combine 1¼ cup (150 g) powdered sugar, 4 teaspoons (20 ml) milk, and ½ teaspoon maple extract until smooth. Spread evenly over scones.

Combine remaining powdered sugar with milk. Drizzle over the maple-glazed scones.

Mocha Chocolate Fudge Cakes

YIELD: 5 SERVINGS

These gooey desserts are also known as "pudding cakes." The cocoa-espresso topping poured over the cakes magically combines with the batter as it bakes. The result is a luscious, rich fudginess similar to a molten cake.

¾ cup (100 grams) Kumquat's Gluten-Free All-Purpose Flour Blend (page 15) or gluten-free all-purpose flour

½ cup (112 g) plus 1 tablespoon (14 g) cocoa powder, divided

1 tablespoon (5.4 g) plus ¼ teaspoon instant espresso powder, divided

1½ teaspoons (7 g) baking powder

½ teaspoon cinnamon

¼ teaspoon salt

1 cup (200 g) sugar

¼ cup (55 g) butter, softened

3 large eggs

1 teaspoon vanilla extract

2 ounces (57 g) bittersweet chocolate (60 percent cacao), finely chopped

Cooking spray

⅓ cup (75 g) packed brown sugar

¼ cup (60 ml) hot water

Powdered sugar, for sprinkling

Preheat oven to 350°F (180°C, or gas mark 4).

Combine the flour, ½ cup (112 g) cocoa powder, 1 tablespoon (5.4 g) espresso powder, baking powder, cinnamon, and salt in a medium bowl.

Combine the sugar and butter in another medium bowl and beat with an electric mixer for 1 minute or until well blended. Add the eggs and vanilla and then beat for 2 minutes. Stir the flour mixture into the egg mixture. Stir in the chopped chocolate.

Spoon the batter into 5 (3½-ounce, or 105 ml) ramekins coated with cooking spray. Place the ramekins on a baking sheet.

Combine the remaining cocoa powder, espresso powder, brown sugar, and water in a bowl. Pour the mixture evenly over the batter in the ramekins, but do not stir.

Bake for 15 to 18 minutes or until the edges are set and the centers are soft. Sprinkle lightly with powdered sugar, if desired. Serve immediately.

Peanut Butter & Chocolate-Covered Raisin Bars

YIELD: 16 BAR COOKIES

These are precisely the types of treats I wish I could have ready every day at about three o'clock in the afternoon. That's right when the afternoon begins to drag, my sugar and caffeine cravings hit, and I need a little pick-me-up. These naturally gluten-free cookie bars are chocolaty and chewy in all of the best ways.

Cooking spray
¼ cup (55 g) butter, softened
½ cup (115 g) packed brown sugar
½ cup (100 g) sugar
1 cup (260 g) peanut butter
2 large eggs
1 teaspoon vanilla extract
2¼ cups (205 grams) gluten-free rolled oats
1 teaspoon baking soda
⅛ teaspoon salt
1½ cups (270 g) gluten-free chocolate-covered raisins, such as Raisinets

Preheat oven to 350°F (180°C, or gas mark 4).

Line a 9-inch (23 cm) baking pan with parchment paper, leaving a 2-inch (5-cm) overhang around the sides. Coat the parchment with cooking spray.

Beat the butter at medium speed with an electric mixer until creamy. Add the sugars and beat well. Add the peanut butter, eggs, and vanilla and beat well. Add the oats, baking soda, and salt and stir well. Stir in the chocolate-covered raisins.

Press the mixture evenly into the prepared pan. Bake for 27 minutes or until golden brown. Cool slightly. Lift the bars from the pan using the overhang of parchment. Cut into 16 squares.

✹ RECIPE TIP: KNOW YOUR OATS ✹

Always confirm that your oats are certified gluten-free. Oats are frequently processed in facilities that also process wheat, so chances of cross-contamination are very high. There are, however, several companies that produce oats and oat products that are certified gluten-free. If you have a reason to be concerned, check with your doctor before consuming oats.

Piña Colada Cupcakes

YIELD: 12 CUPCAKES

I love using coconut flour. It adds a fragrant and delicious natural coconut flavor to these cupcakes and is also high in fiber and protein. What's a better flavor combination than pineapple and rum?

FOR CUPCAKES:
¾ cup (about 100 grams) coconut flour
⅔ cup (about 90 grams) Kumquat's Gluten-Free All-Purpose Flour Blend (page 15) or gluten-free all-purpose flour
1½ teaspoons (7 g) baking powder
½ teaspoon salt
½ cup (120 ml) pineapple juice
12 tablespoons (1½ sticks, or 167 g) butter
1 tablespoon (15 ml) dark rum
3 large eggs, room temperature
¾ cup plus 2½ teaspoons (170 grams) sugar

FOR GLAZE:
1¼ cups (150 g) powdered sugar
5 teaspoons (25 ml) pineapple juice
Turbinado sugar, for sprinkling

To make the cupcakes: Preheat oven to 350°F (180°C, or gas mark 4).

Line 12 muffin tins with cupcake wrappers. Combine the coconut flour, all-purpose flour, baking powder, and salt in a medium bowl.

Heat the pineapple juice, butter, and rum in a medium saucepan over medium-high heat until the butter melts. Meanwhile, beat the eggs and sugar in the bowl of a standing mixer on high speed until thick and pale, about 5 minutes. Quickly beat in the flour, being careful to not deflate the eggs. Quickly add the pineapple juice mixture to the batter and beat until smooth.

Divide the mixture evenly among the cupcake wrappers using an ice cream scoop. Quickly and gently shake the muffin pan from side to side to even the batter in the wrappers. Bake the cupcakes for 22 minutes or until lightly golden. Cool on a rack.

To make the glaze: Combine the powdered sugar and pineapple juice and then whisk until smooth. Add more sugar or more juice to make a thick, but spreadable glaze. Top the cooled cupcakes evenly with the glaze. Sprinkle with turbinado sugar.

> ✳ RECIPE TIP: GIVE YOUR GLAZE A PUNCH ✳
>
> For a boozy glaze, substitute 2 teaspoons (10 ml) rum for 2 teaspoons (10 ml) of the pineapple juice before adding to the powdered sugar.

Pumpkin-Chocolate Chip Muffins

YIELD: 12 MUFFINS

When we were all single, two of my dearest friends and I made an effort to travel to see each other. Every time we ended up at the home of my friend in Nashville, we'd hit our favorite local coffee shop in the mornings, always ordering huge cups of coffee and pumpkin–chocolate chip muffins. It became a ritual we had to keep. So, just for them I've developed these.

1½ cups (210 grams) Kumquat's Gluten-Free All-Purpose Flour Blend (page 15) or gluten-free all-purpose flour
1 teaspoon baking powder
1 teaspoon baking soda
1 teaspoon pumpkin pie spice
1 teaspoon cinnamon
½ teaspoon salt
½ cup (120 ml) canola oil
1 cup (225 g) packed brown sugar
1 cup (245 g) canned pumpkin
2 large eggs
1 teaspoon vanilla extract
1 cup (175 g) miniature chocolate chips

Preheat oven to 400°F (200°C, or gas mark 6).

Line 12 muffin tins with cupcake wrappers.

Combine the flour, baking powder, baking soda, pumpkin pie spice, cinnamon, and salt in a large bowl. Combine the oil, brown sugar, pumpkin, eggs, and vanilla in a medium bowl. Stir the oil mixture into the flour mixture until combined. Stir in the chocolate chips.

Spoon the mixture evenly into the muffin pan. Bake for 21 minutes and then cool on a rack.

✸ RECIPE TIP: MAKE YOUR OWN SPICE BLEND ✸

Pumpkin pie spice is just a combination of cinnamon, ginger, nutmeg, allspice, and cloves. If you don't have the blend, you can combine your own.

Soft & Chewy Snickerdoodles

YIELD: 27 COOKIES

Some of the first cookies that I remember baking religiously in my mother's kitchen were snickerdoodles. I still have the recipe proudly written in my little-girl handwriting in my very old, orange recipe book. These buttery, chewy, cinnamon-scented cookies are completely gratifying and will make your house smell heavenly as they bake.

1 teaspoon golden flaxseed meal
2 teaspoons (10 ml) very hot water
½ cup (100 g) shortening
½ cup (1 stick, or 112 g) butter, softened
1½ cups (300 g) plus 2½ tablespoons (32.5 g) sugar, divided
1 tablespoon (15 ml) corn syrup
2 large eggs
1 large egg yolk
2 teaspoons (10 ml) vanilla extract
3¼ cups plus 1 tablespoon (about 425 grams) Kumquat's Gluten-Free All-Purpose Flour Blend (page 15) or gluten-free all-purpose flour
2 teaspoons (9 g) cream of tartar
1 teaspoon baking soda
½ teaspoon salt
3¼ teaspoons (7.5 g) cinnamon, divided

Preheat oven to 375°F (190°C, or gas mark 5).

Combine the flaxseed meal and water in a small bowl; stir until a slurry forms. Set aside.

Cream together the shortening and butter with an electric mixer in a large bowl. Add 1½ cups (300 g) sugar and then cream together for 1 minute. Beat in the corn syrup, whole eggs, egg yolk, and vanilla. Beat in the flax slurry.

Combine the flour, cream of tartar, baking soda, salt, and ¼ teaspoon cinnamon in a medium bowl. Add the flour mixture to the shortening mixture and mix until combined (dough will be a bit soft, but not sticky). Roll the dough into 2-inch (5 cm) balls.

Combine the remaining sugar and remaining cinnamon in a small bowl. Roll the cookie balls in the cinnamon-sugar mixture. Place the balls on a baking sheet lined with parchment paper and then press the balls to ½-inch (12 mm) thickness. Bake for 11 minutes, or until the edges are set and the center is just slightly soft. Cool for 3 minutes on the baking sheet and then remove to a rack to cool.

Triple Chocolate Truffle Brownies

YIELD: 9 TO 12 SERVINGS

We all need a chocolate fix every once in a while. And these indulgent brownies will fix you three times over. If you like a fudgy, gooey, mouthful of chocolate, stop what you're doing and bake these now.

¾ cup (1½ sticks, or 167 g) butter
4 ounces (114 g) bittersweet chocolate (60 percent cacao), finely chopped
3 large eggs
1 cup (235 ml) sugar
¼ teaspoon salt
1 teaspoon vanilla extract
¾ cup plus 2 tablespoons (105 grams) Kumquat's Gluten-Free All-Purpose Flour Blend (page 15) or gluten-free all-purpose flour
½ cup (64 g) cocoa powder
½ cup (90 g) coarsely chopped white chocolate
½ cup (90 g) coarsely chopped milk chocolate

Preheat oven to 350°F (180°C, or gas mark 4).

Line a 9-inch (23 cm) baking pan with parchment paper.

Heat the butter and bittersweet chocolate in a medium bowl in the microwave on HIGH for 30 seconds; stir well. Heat for an additional 30 seconds on HIGH; stir well until melted. Set aside.

Beat the eggs, sugar, and salt on high speed with a standing or electric mixer for 3 minutes or until light and fluffy. Stir in the vanilla. Stir in the chocolate mixture, flour, and cocoa powder. Fold in the white and milk chocolates.

Pour the mixture into the prepared baking pan and bake for 26 minutes or until the edges are done and the middle is just set.

White Chocolate, Coconut, Lime & Pecan Blondies

YIELD: 16 SERVINGS

Years ago I developed a blondie with white chocolate and lime. Over time, friends and I have been adding things to the bowl that have resulted in the ultimate blondie. This flavor combination is so incredibly drool-worthy and delightful.

¾ cup (1½ sticks, or 167 g) butter, melted
1 cup (225 g) packed brown sugar
3 large eggs
2 teaspoons (10 ml) vanilla extract
1 cup (140 grams) Kumquat's Gluten-Free All-Purpose Flour Blend (page 15) or gluten-free all-purpose flour
¼ teaspoon salt
½ cup (88 g) white chocolate chunks or morsels
½ cup (55 g) chopped pecans
⅓ cup (40 g) dried cranberries
⅓ cup (28 g) sweetened, shredded coconut
1 tablespoon (6 g) organic lime zest
Cooking spray

Preheat oven to 350°F (180°C, or gas mark 4).

Line a 9-inch (23 cm) square baking pan with parchment paper.

Mix together the butter, brown sugar, eggs, and vanilla in a medium bowl. Add the flour and salt to the butter mixture and stir until the batter is smooth and well combined. Fold in the white chocolate morsels, pecans, cranberries, coconut, and lime zest.

Pour the batter into the prepared pan. Bake for 26 minutes or until a wooden skewer or pick inserted in the center comes out clean. Cool on a rack.

Gingerbread Fig Loaf

I am always happy to have fresh gingerbread in the house, and I believe it shouldn't only be appreciated during the holidays. Not to mention, quick breads like this one are so easy to stir, dump, and bake that you have no excuse to not make it.

2 cups (about 280 grams) Kumquat's Gluten-Free All-Purpose Flour Blend (page 15) or gluten-free all-purpose flour

1 teaspoon ground ginger

1 teaspoon cinnamon

1 teaspoon baking soda

½ teaspoon baking powder

¼ teaspoon ground cloves

¼ teaspoon salt

⅔ cup (163 g) applesauce

⅓ cup (113 g) molasses

2 large eggs

½ cup (115 g) packed brown sugar

½ cup (1 stick, or 112 g) butter, melted

1 teaspoon vanilla extract

1 cup (150 g) dried Mission figs, halved lengthwise

Cooking spray

Preheat oven to 350°F (180°C, or gas mark 4).

Combine the flour, ginger, cinnamon, baking soda, baking powder, cloves, and salt in a large bowl.

Combine the applesauce, molasses, eggs, brown sugar, butter, and vanilla in a medium bowl. Add the applesauce mixture to the flour mixture and stir to combine. Fold in the figs.

Pour the batter into an 8-inch (20 cm) loaf pan coated with cooking spray. Bake for 55 minutes or until a wooden skewer or pick inserted into the center of the loaf comes out clean. Cool in the pan on a rack.

Resources

>>> Helpful Websites <<<

NATIONAL FOUNDATION FOR CELIAC AWARENESS
www.celiaccentral.org

CELIAC DISEASE FOUNDATION
www.celiac.org

AMERICAN CELIAC DISEASE ALLIANCE
www.americanceliac.org

GLUTEN INTOLERANCE GROUP OF NORTH AMERICA
www.gluten.net

CELIAC SPRUE ASSOCIATION
www.csaceliacs.info

CELIAC DISEASE AWARENESS CAMPAIGN OF THE NATIONAL INSTITUTES OF HEALTH
www.celiac.nih.gov

KUMQUAT (MY BLOG)
www.kumquatblog.com

>>> My Preferred Pantry Brands <<<

FLOURS: I use mostly Bob's Red Mill gluten-free flours and Authentic Foods superfine brown rice flour. I am also a fan of King Arthur gluten-free multipurpose flour.

PASTA: Jovial pasta is my favorite by far. Tinkyada rice pasta is my second choice.

FLAXSEED MEAL: I use Bob's Red Mill golden flaxseed meal.

BROTHS: I use Pacific Natural Foods broths.

Acknowledgments

The opportunity I've been given to author my own cookbook is one I never expected to have. There are so many fantastic people to whom I owe tremendous thanks and eternal gratitude.

A heaping helping of thank-yous go to Amanda Waddell, Will Kiester, Meg Sniegoski, and all of the others at Fair Winds Press. What a gift of an opportunity you've placed in my hands. Thank you.

Like all of the sparkly gowned, award-winning actresses on Oscar night, I feel there are just so many to thank. What would we be without amazing friends surrounding us, supporting us, and making us laugh through all of the moments of life? Thank you, dear Regan Jones, for doing all of those things on an almost daily basis. It's been fun riding these rides with you and seeing sneak peeks of the future. Thanks to my most generous neighbor, friend, and faithful taste tester, Kelly Trout, for graciously accepting large amounts of food and always giving honest and gentle feedback in return. Carrie, Amanda, Elaine, Kirsten, Cynthia, Jill, and Berit . . . thanks for loving me and being merely a phone call away.

I am incredibly blessed with an amazing family, and it is important for me to take a pause to let them know. Thank you, dear sister, for testing my recipes and being my cheerleader. Thanks to my mother-in-law, Nancy, for the days of childcare, for telling me my food is good, and for reminding me of "the Little Engine that Could" on the challenging days. I owe buckets and buckets of thanks to my loving parents. To Dad for beaming with pride and selling the book before it's even printed. To my beautiful Mom for countless recipes tested, manuscripts read, encouragement given, and prayers offered. To you, my love, thank you for the patience, the quiet support, and the unknown number of hours you entertained our son while I hunched over the stove, the sink, the photo set, and the computer. To my sweet boy, thanks for bringing joy, smiles, and bad-guy sword-fighting into my every day. And thanks for being a good eater. I love you.

And thank you to my infinitely creative Father who holds all things together. Thank you for gifting me with a smidge of your creativity and for allowing me to share it with others. Bless them. Give them hope and health.

Special Thanks to My Recipe Testers

Adina Pease, Alysa Bajenaru, Amanda Koch, Anna Courie, Carrie Zarechnak, Clare Minges, Cynthia Roelle, E. A. Stewart, Elaine Case, Emily Teufel, Emma Cutfield, Jeannine Smith, Jenifer Humphries, Kelly Trout, Kimberly Collins, Kirsten Braatz, Laura Hurlburt, Leah Stewart, Lisa Martin, Marissa Farrell, Melinda Buchanan, Melissa Brooker, Meredith Neill, Pam Pailes, Regan Jones, Sarah Dawson, Susan Feldtman, Teresa Raymond, Tracey Linneweber, and Tricia Loughridge.

Millions and millions of thanks to those close friends and family, and those generous readers of my blog, who tested these recipes for me and generally showed me constant kindness. I am humbled and grateful that you stepped up to the plate to help me with this project. I can't say it enough . . . Thank you for supporting me!

Some Tester Reviews

Carrot Cake Pancakes with Cream Cheese Frosting: "I love the idea of carrot cake pancakes—gluten-free and healthy to boot! These have a delicious flavor and slightly crunchy texture, plus the cream cheese icing adds a little touch of decadence!" **E. A. Stewart**

Hot Quinoa Cereal with Blueberries and Pecans: "The hot quinoa cereal is the perfect cure for 'oatmeal O.D.' It is pleasantly sweet, delicious, and certain to find a permanent place in your breakfast rotation." **Kimberly Collins**

Sweet Potato Hash with Ham: "It was amazing and had such wonderful, complex flavors. My husband, who doesn't like sweet potatoes or ham, cleaned his plate. And my 11-month-old inhaled it. An added plus was it was already in bite-size pieces so required no extra work on my part to make it work for her." **Sarah Dawson**

Mango Guacamole: "Gretchen's fresh take on guacamole, transforms classic condiment into the star of any meal. It's so delicious and full of flavor, tortilla chips are totally unnecessary—go for a spoon instead!" **Kelly Trout**

Coconut-Almond Hot Chocolate: "The combination of coconut milk and almond extract create a fresh flavor that rivals the traditional addition of peppermint. It's rich, indulgent, and really is chocolate at its best!" **Adina Pease**

Pecan-Crusted Chicken Tenders: "Super tasty chicken tenders with just enough spice but still not too much spice for kids. Simple, quick, and healthy! A definite recipe to add to our weekly menu!" **Melissa Brooker**

Spaghetti and Meatballs: "It was quick, easy & delicious… my kind of recipe. I heard the words tonight that every mom wants to hear at dinner: 'Can I have seconds?'" **Lisa Martin**

Rustic Italian Salad with Grilled Chicken: "This recipe was YUMMY! We all enjoyed it. The kids were still talking about it the next day, asking when we could have it for dinner again." **Alysa Bajenaru**

Tarragon-Lemon Chicken Salad: "This recipe puts all the other chicken salads to shame. Fresh ingredients create memorable food. You won't use dried herbs in a chicken salad again!" **Emma Cutfield**

Chocolate Chili: "It tasted great, and the chocolate did a nice job giving the chili some richness and silkiness without making it overly sweet." **Meredith Neill**

Red Curry Chicken Soup: "You know your soup is a hit when your children not only lick the bowl clean but also beg you to make it again!" **Laura Hurlburt**

Indian-Spiced Peas: "Peas don't have to be boring!! These jazzy, zippy babies have an exotic flair... and the carrots provide just the right amount of crunch. So easy to make, I will have them all the time." **Jeannine Smith**

Orange Biscuits: "Yum! In my family's words, 'When are we making it again?'" **Pam Pailes**

Bananas with Caramel-Chocolate Sauce: "I loved the taste and texture of the bananas. It has the perfect chocolate/caramel balance. One of my boys said, 'It's like a chocolate party in my mouth!'" **Jenifer Humphries**

Cinnamon-Almond Cookies: "So pretty. So easy. So yummy." **Susan Feldtman**

Caramel Apple Galettes: "They were DELICIOUS. My plan was to save them for dessert after dinner tonight, but they looked and smelled so good, we couldn't resist so hubby and I just split one after a few minutes of cooling." **Melinda Buchanan**

Pumpkin–Chocolate Chip Muffins: "The flavor was perfectly balanced. I really like using the mini chocolate chips because it seemed there was more chocolate in every bite—not just hunting and pecking for the bigger chips." **Carrie Zarechnak**

About
the Author

GRETCHEN F. BROWN, R.D., is the founder of www.kumquatblog.com, a gluten-free blog devoted to the belief that gluten-free food can and should be easy to prepare, wholesome, and delicious enough for everyone.

Gretchen has worked in the test kitchens and photography studios of Oxmoor House and is now a freelance recipe developer, food stylist, food writer, and food photographer. She has been gluten-free for several years, as a result of a lifetime of stomach pains and health problems.

She lives with her husband and son in Charlottesville, Virginia.

Index